"Publish this Work ("The Poem of the Man-God ") as it is. It is not necessary to give any opinion about its origin or whether it can be extraordinary or not. Whoever reads it, will understand"

His Holiness Pope Pius XII,
February 26, 1948.

1

Code Of Canon Law

Canon 66 «The Christian economy, therefore, since it is the new and definitive Covenant, will never pass away; and no new public revelation is to be expected before the glorious manifestation of our Lord Jesus Christ." Yet even if Revelation is already complete, it has not been made completely explicit; it remains for Christian faith gradually to grasp its full significance over the course of the centuries.

Canon 67 Throughout the ages, there have been so-called «private» revelations, some of which have been recognized by the authority of the Church. They do not belong, however, to the deposit of faith. It is not their role to improve or complete Christ's definitive Revelation, but to help live more fully by it in a certain period of history. Guided by the Magisterium of the Church, the sensus fidelium knows how to discern and welcome in these revelations whatever constitutes an authentic call of Christ or his saints to the Church.

Christian faith cannot accept "revelations" that claim to surpass or correct the Revelation of which Christ is the fulfilment, as is the case in certain non-Christian religions and also in certain recent sects which base themselves on such "revelations."

The Full Of Grace:
The Early Years.
The Merit.
Joseph's Passion.
The Blue Angel.
The Boyhood Of Jesus.

Follow Me:
Treasure With 7 Names
Where There Are Thorns, There Also Will Be Roses
For Love That Perseveres
The Apostolic College
The Decalogue

The Chronicles Of Jesus & Judas Iscariot:
I See You As You Are
Those Who Are Marked
Jesus Weeps

Lazarus:
That Beautiful Blonde
Flowers Of Bounty

Claudia Procula:
Do You Love The Nazarene?
The Caprice Of Court Morals

Christian Tenets:
On Reincarnation

Mary Of Magdala:
Ah! My Beloved! I Reached You At Last!

Lamb Books
Illustrated adaptations for the whole family

LAMB BOOKS

Published by Lamb Books, 2 Dalkeith Court, 45 Vincent Street, London SW1P 4HH;

UK, USA, FR, IT, SP, PT, DE

www.lambbooks.org

First published by Lamb Books 2013
This edition
001
Text copyright @ Lamb Books Nominee, 2013
Illustrations copyright @ Lamb Books, 2013
The moral right of the author and illustrator has been asserted
All rights reserved

The author and publisher are grateful to the Centro Editoriale Valtoriano in Italy for Permission to quote from the Poem of the Man- God by Maria Valtorta, by Valtorta Publishing

Set in Palatino Linotype R
Printed and bound by CPI Group (UK) Ltd, Croydon, CR0, 4YY

Follow Me

For Love That Perseveres

LAMBBOOKS

Acknowledgements

The material in this book is adapted from 'The Poem of the Man+God' (The Gospel As Revealed To Me) by Maria Valtorta, first approved by Pope Pius XII in 1948, when, in a meeting on February 26th 1948, witnessed by three other priests, he ordered the three priest present to "Publish this work as it is".

In 1994, the Vatican heeded to the calls of Christians worldwide and have begun to examine the case for the Canonization of Maria Valtorta (Little John).

The Poem of the Man God was described by Pope Pius' confessor as "edifying". Mystical revelations have long been the province of priests and the religious. Now, they are accessible to all. May all who read this adaptation, also find it edifying. And through this light, may Faith be renewed.

Special Thanks to the Centro Editoriale Valtortiano in Italy for permission to quote from the Poem of the Man God by Maria Valtorta, nick named, Little John.

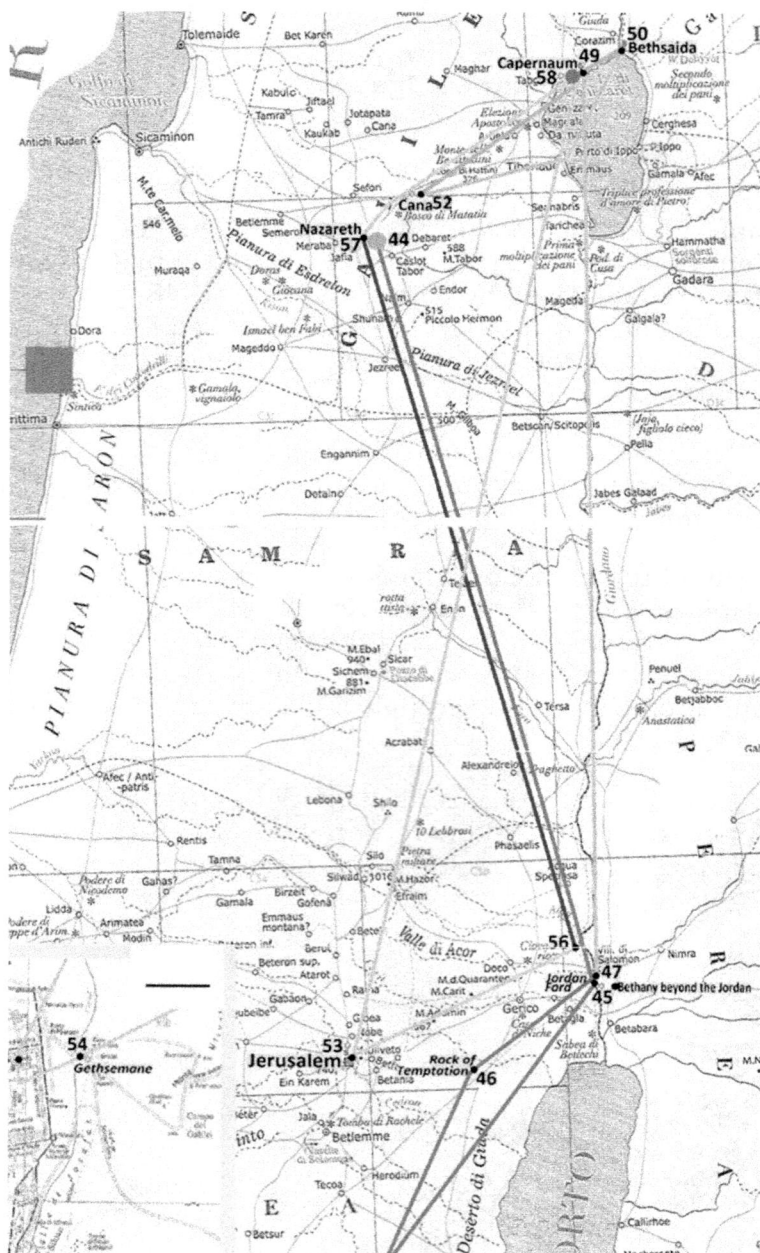

For Love That Perseveres

Follow Me

Contents

Jesus, John, Simon And Judas Go To Bethlehem

Jesus, Who is already with John, meets Simon and Judas, early in the morning, at the same gate in Jerusalem.

'My friends...' says Jesus '...I ask you to come with Me through Judaea. If it is not too much for you, particularly for you, Simon.'

'Why, Master?'

'It is hard to walk on the Judaean mountains... and perhaps it will be even more painful for you to meet someone who harmed you.'

'As far as the road is concerned, I wish to assure You, once again, that since You cured me, I feel stronger than a young man and no work is heavy for me, also because it is done for You, and now, with You. With regard to meeting people who harmed me, there is no harsh resentment or feeling in Simon's heart, since he became Yours. Hatred has gone together with the scales of the disease. And believe me, I cannot tell You whether You worked a greater miracle in curing my corroded flesh or my soul consumed by hatred. I do not think I am wrong in saying the curing my soul was the greater miracle; A wound of the soul heals less easily... and You cured me in one instant. That is a miracle. Because one does not recover all of a sudden, even if one wants to with all of one's strength and a man does not get rid of a bad moral habit, if You do not destroy that habit with Your sanctifying will power.'

'Your judgment is correct.'

'Why do You not do that with everyone? 'asks Judas, somewhat resentfully.

'But He does, Judas...' put in John, laying a kind and loving arm on Judas as though to calm him down and speaking anxiously and persuasively '... Why do you speak like that to the Master? Do you not feel you have changed since you have been in contact with Him? Previously, I was a disciple of John the Baptist. But I have found myself completely changed since He said to me: "Come".'

John, who seldom interferes, and never does in the presence of the Master, finds himself compelled to speak but then realises he has spoken before Jesus, blushes and says:

'Forgive me, Master, I spoke in Your stead, but I wanted... I did not want Judas to grieve You.'

'Yes, John. But he did not grieve Me as My disciple. When he is My disciple, then, if he persists in his way of thinking, he will grieve Me. It grieves Me only to notice how much man has been corrupted by Satan who perverts his thoughts. All men, you know! The thoughts of all of you have been misled by him! But the day will come, when you will have the Strength and the Grace of God, you will have Wisdom with His Spirit... you will then have everything to enable you to judge rightly.'

'And will we all judge rightly.'

'No, Judas.'

'But are You referring to us, disciples, or to all men?'

'I refer firstly to you, and to all the others. When the time comes, the Master will nominate His workers and send them all over the world...'

'Are You not doing that already?'

'For the time being, I use you only to say: "The Messiah is here. Come to Him." Later I will make you capable of preaching in My name, of working miracles in My name...'

'Oh! Also miracles?'

'Yes, on bodies and on souls.'

'Oh! How they will admire us, then! ' exhales Judas, overjoyed at the thought.

'But, then, we shall not be with the Master... and I will always be afraid to do with my human capacity what comes only from God 'says John, looking thoughtfully and somewhat sadly at Jesus.

'John, if the Master will allow me, I would like to tell you what I think 'says Simon.

'Yes, tell John. I want you to advise one another.'

'Do You already know it is advice?' Jesus smiles and is quiet.

'Well, I tell you, John, that you must not, we must not be afraid. Let us found upon His wisdom of a holy Master and upon His promise. If He says: "I will send you", it means that He knows that He can send us without any fear that we may do harm to Him or to ourselves, that is to the cause of God, that is so dear to each of us, like a newly-wed bride. If He promises to clothe our intellectual and spiritual misery with the brightness of the power His Father gives Him for us, we must be

certain that He will do so and that we will be successful,
not by ourselves, but through His mercy. All this will
most certainly happen, providing our deeds are free
from pride and human ambitions. I think that if we
contaminate our mission, which is entirely a spiritual
one, with earthly ingredients, then also Christ's promise
will no longer stand. Not because of any inability on His
part, but because we will strangle such ability with the
rope of pride. I do not know whether I have made myself
understood.'

'You have spoken very clearly. I am wrong. But you
know... I think that after all, to wish to be admired as the
Messiah's disciples, so close to Him as to deserve to do
what He does, is the same as wishing to increase even
more the powerful figure of Christ among people. Praise
to the Master, Who has such disciples, that is what I
mean' answers Judas.

'What you say is not entirely wrong. But... see, Judas.
I come from a caste which is persecuted because...
because it misunderstood what and how the Messiah
should be. Yes. If we had waited for Him with the correct
vision of His being, we would not have fallen into errors,
which blaspheme against the Truth and rebel against
the Law of Rome, so that we have been punished both by
God and by Rome. We fancied Christ as a conqueror who
would free Israel, as a new Maccabaeus, greater than
the great Judas... Only that. And why? Because rather
than have regard to the interest of God we took care of
our own interests: of the fatherland and of the people.
Oh! The interests of the fatherland are most certainly
sacred. But what are they when compared to the eternal
Heavens? In the long hours of persecution, first, and then

of isolation, when as a fugitive, I was compelled to hide in
the dens of wild beasts, sharing food and bed with them,
to escape Roman power and above all the impeachments
of false friends; or when, whilst waiting for death in the
cave of a leper, I already had a foretaste of the savour
of the sepulchre, how much did I meditate, and how
much did I see: I saw the figure of the Messiah... Yours,
my humble and good Master, Yours, Master and King of
the Spirit, Yours, O Christ, Son of the Father, leading to
the Father, and not to the royal palaces of dust, nor to
the deities of mud. You... Oh! It is easy for me to follow
You... Because, forgive my daring which avows itself to be
correct, because I see You as I thought of You, I recognise
You, I recognised You at once. No, it was not a question
of meeting You, but of recognising One whom my soul
had already met...'

'That is why I called you... and that is why I am taking
you with Me, now, in this first journey of Mine in Judaea.
I want you to complete your recognition... and I want
also these, whom age makes less capable of reaching
the Truth by means of deep meditation, I want them to
know how their Master has come to this hour... You will
understand later. There is David's Tower. The Eastern
Gate is near.'

'Are we going out by it?'

'Yes, Judas. We are going to Bethlehem first. Where I
was born... You ought to know... to tell the others. Also
that is part of the knowledge of the Messiah and of the
Scriptures. You will find prophecies written in things not
as prophecies but as history. Let us go round Herod's
houses...'

'The old, wicked, lustful fox.'

'Do not judge. There is God, Who judges. Let us go along the path through these vegetable gardens. We will stop under the shade of a tree, near some hospitable house, until it cools down. Then we will go on our way.'

Jesus At Bethlehem In The Peasant's House And In The Grotto

It is a hot dry summer day on a flat road covered in dust and stones, running along an Olive grove of huge olive trees laden with small newly formed olives. Where it has not been trodden, the ground is strewn with minute olive flowers shaken to the ground during pollination.
Keeping in the shade of the olive trees and away from the worst of the dust, Jesus with His three disciples proceed in a single along the edge of the road where the grass is still green, following it as it turns in a right angle where there is a closed and abandoned square building surmounted by a little low dome. From there, it is an easy climb into a large horseshoe shaped valley strewn with houses forming a small town.

'That is Rachel's sepulchre' says Simon.
'In that case, we have almost arrived. Are we going into town at once?'
'No, Judas, I want to show you a place first... Then we will go into town, and since there is still clear daylight and it will be an evening of moonlight, we will be able to speak to the people. If they will listen to us.'
'Do You think they will not listen to You?'

They reach the sepulchre, an ancient whitewashed and well preserved monument.

Jesus stops to drink at a rustic well nearby. A woman who has come to draw water offers Him some.

'Are you from Bethlehem?' Jesus asks her.

'I am. But now at harvest time, I live in the country here with my husband, to look after the vegetable gardens and the orchards. Are You Galilean?'

'I was born in Bethlehem, but I live at Nazareth in Galilee.'

'Are You persecuted, too?'

'The family is. But why do you say: "You too"? Are there many people persecuted among the Bethlehemites?'

'Don't You know? What age are You?'

'Thirty.'

'Then You were born exactly when... oh! what a calamity! But why was He born here?'

'Who?'

'The One they said was the Saviour. Cursed be the fools who, drunk as they were, thought the clouds were angels and the bleating and braying were voices from Heaven, and in their drunken haze mistook three miserable people for the holiest people on the earth. Cursed be they! And cursed be those who believe them.'

'But, with all your cursing, you are not telling Me what happened. Why are you cursing?'

'Because... Listen: where are You going?'

'To Bethlehem with My friends. I have business there. I must visit some old friends and take them the greetings of My Mother. But I would like to know many things before, because we have been away, we of the family, for many years. We left the town when I was only a few months old.'

'Before the catastrophe, then. Listen, if You do not loathe the house of a peasant, come and share our bread and salt with us. You and Your companions. We will talk during supper and I will put you all up for the night. My house is small. But above the stable there is a lot of hay, all piled up. The night is clear and warm. If You want, You can sleep there.'

'May the Lord of Israel reward your hospitality. I will be happy to come to your house.'

'A pilgrim brings blessings with him. Let us go. But I shall have to pour six jars of water on the vegetables which have just come up.'

'And I will help you.'

'No, You are a gentleman, Your behaviour says so.'

'I am a worker, woman. This one is a fisherman. Those two Judaeans are well off and employed. I am not.' And He picks up a jar which was lying flat on its big belly near the very low wall of the well, He ties it to the rope, and lowers it into the well. John helps Him. Also the others wish to be as helpful and they ask the woman: 'Where are the vegetables? Tell us and we will take the jars there.'

'May God bless you! My back is broken with fatigue. Come...'

And while Jesus is pulling up His jar, the three disciples disappear along a little path... and come back with two empty ones, which they fill up and then go away. And they do not do that three, but ten times. And Judas laughing says: 'She is shouting herself hoarse, blessing us. We have given so much water to her salad that the soil will be damp for at least two days, and the woman

will not have to break her back. 'When he comes back for
the last time, he says: 'Master, I am afraid we have been
unlucky.'

'Why, Judas?'

'Because she has it in for the Messiah. I said to her:
"Don't curse. Don't you know that the Messiah is the
greatest grace for the people of God? Yahweh promised
Him to Jacob, and after him to all the Prophets and the
just people in Israel. And you hate Him?" She replied:
"Not Him. But the one whom some drunken shepherds
and three cursed diviners from the East called 'Messiah'
". And since that is You...'

'It does not matter. I know I am placed as a trial and
contradiction for many. Did you tell her who I am?'

'No, I am not a fool. I wanted to save Your back and ours.'

'You did well. Not because of our backs. But because I
wish to show Myself when I think the time is right. Let us
go.'

Judas leads Him as far as the vegetable garden.

The woman empties the last three jars and then takes
Him towards a rustic building in the middle of the
orchard. 'Go in...', she says '...my husband is already in
the house.'

They look into a low smoky kitchen. 'Peace be to this
house 'greets Jesus.

'Whoever You are, may You and Your friends be blessed.
Come in', replies the man. And he takes a basin of water
out to them to refresh and clean themselves after which
they all go in and sit round a rough table.

'Thank you for helping my wife. She told me. I had never
dealt with Galileans before and I was told that they are
rough and quarrelsome. But you have been kind and

good. Although already tired... you worked so hard. Are
you coming from far?'
'From Jerusalem. These two are Judaeans. The other one
and I are from Galilee. But, believe Me, man: you will find
good and bad everywhere.'
'That's true. I, the first time I have met Galileans, I have
found them to be good. Woman: bring the food. I have
but bread, vegetables, olives and cheese. I am a peasant.'
'I am not a gentleman Myself. I am a carpenter.'
'What? You? With Your manners?'
The woman intervenes: 'Our guest is from Bethlehem, I
told you, and if His relations are persecuted, they were
probably rich and learned, like Joshua of Ur, Matthew of
Isaac, Levi of Abraham, poor people!...'
'You have not been questioned. Forgive her. Women are
more talkative than sparrows in the evening.'
'Were they Bethlehemite families?'
'What? You do not know who they are, and You come
from Bethlehem?'
'We ran away when I was a few months old... 'but the
talkative woman interrupts 'He went away before the
massacre.'
'Eh! I see that. Otherwise He would not be in this world.
Have You never been back?'
'No, never.'
'What a calamity! You will not find many of those Sarah
said You want to meet and visit. Many were killed, many
ran away, many... who knows!... missing, and it has
never been known whether they died in the desert or
were killed in jail as a punishment for their rebellion. But
was it a rebellion? And who would have remained
inactive allowing so many innocents to be slaughtered?

No, it is unfair that Levi and Elias should still be alive
when so many innocents are dead!'
'Who are those two, and what did they do?'
'Well... at least You will have heard of the slaughter. The
slaughter by Herod... Over a thousand babies
slaughtered in town, almost another thousand in the
country. And they were all, or almost all, males, because
in their fury, in the darkness, in the scuffle, the killers
tore away from their cradles, from their mother's beds,
from the houses they assailed, also some baby girls, and
they pierced them like sucking baby gazelles shot down
by archers. Well: why all that? Because a group of
shepherds, who had obviously drank a huge quantity of
cider to withstand the intense night cold, in a frenzy of
excitement, stated they had seen angels, heard songs,
received instructions... and they said to us of Bethlehem:
"Come. Adore. The Messiah is born." Just imagine: the
Messiah in a cave! In all sincerity, I must admit that we
were all drunk, even I, then an adolescent, also my wife,
then only a few years old... because we all believed them,
and in a poor Galilean woman we saw the Virgin Mother
mentioned by the Prophets. But She was with Her
husband, a rough Galilean! If She was the wife, how
could She be the "Virgin"? To cut a long story short: we
believed.
Gifts, worshipping... houses opened to give them
hospitality!...
Oh! They played their roles very well! Poor Anne! She lost
her property and her life, and also the children of her
oldest daughter, the only one left because she was
married to a merchant in Jerusalem, lost all their
property because their house was burned down and the

whole holding was laid waste by Herod's order. Now it is an uncultivated field where herds feed.'

'And was it entirely the shepherds' fault?'

'No, it was the fault also of three wizards who came from Satan's kingdom. Perhaps they were accomplices of the three... And we foolishly felt proud of so much honour! And the poor arch synagogue! We killed him because he swore that the prophecies confirmed the truth of the shepherds' and wizards' words...'

'It was therefore the fault of the shepherds and of the wizards?'

'No, Galilean. It was also our fault. The fault of our credulity. The Messiah had been expected for such a long time! Centuries of expectation. And there had been many recent disappointments because of false Messiahs. One of them was a Galilean, like You, another one was named Theudas. Liars! They... Messiahs! They were nothing but greedy adventurers hunting for a stroke of luck! We should have learned the lesson. Instead...'

'Well, then, why do you curse all the shepherds and magicians? If you consider yourselves fools, too, then you ought to be cursed as well. But the precept of love forbids cursing. One curse attracts another curse. Are you sure you are right? Could it not be true that the shepherds and the magicians spoke the truth, revealed to them by God? Why do you persist in believing they were liars?'

'Because the years of the prophecy were not complete. We thought about it afterwards... after our eyes had been opened by the blood that reddened basins and rivulets.'

'And could the Most High not have advanced the coming of the Saviour, out of an excess of love for His people? On what did the wizards found their statement? You told Me

they came from the East...'
'On their calculations concerning a new star.'
'Is it not written: "A star from Jacob takes the leadership,
a sceptre arises from Israel"? Is Jacob not the great
Patriarch and did he not stop in the land of Bethlehem as
dear to him as his eyes, because his beloved Rachel died
there?
And did the mouth of a Prophet not say: "A shoot springs
from the stock of Jesse, a scion thrusts from his roots"?
Jesse, David's father, was born here. Is the shoot on the
stock, cut at its roots by tyrannical usurpations, is it not
the "Virgin" Who will give birth to Her Son, conceived not
by deed of man, otherwise She would not be a virgin, but
by divine will, whereby He will be the "Immanuel"
because: Son of God, He will be God and bring God
among the people of God, as His name proclaims? And
will He not be announced, as the prophecy says, to the
people walking in darkness, that is to the heathens, "by a
great light"? And the star the magicians saw, could it not
be the star of Jacob, the great light of the two prophecies
of Balaam and Isaiah? And the very massacre ordered by
Herod, does it not come within the prophecies? "A voice
is heard in Ramah... It is Rachel weeping for her
children." It was written that tears should ooze from
Rachel's bones in her sepulchre at Ephrathah when,
through the Saviour, the reward would come to the holy
people. Tears which were to turn into celestial laughter,
just as the rainbow is formed by the last drops of the
storm, but it says: "Here, the sky is clear."'
'You are a learned man. Are You a rabbi?'
'Yes, I am.'
'And I perceived it. There is light and truth in Your words.

But... Oh! too many wounds are still bleeding in this land of Bethlehem because of the true or false Messiah... I would never advise Him to come here. The land would reject Him as it rejects a stepson who caused the death of the true children. In any case... if it was Him... He died with the other slaughtered children.'

'Where do Levi and Elias live now?'

'Do You know them? 'The man becomes suspicious.

'I do not know them. Their faces are unknown to Me. But they are unhappy, and I always have mercy on the unhappy. I want to go and see them.'

'Well, You will be the first one after about thirty years. They are still shepherds and they work for a rich Herodian from Jerusalem, who has taken possession of a lot of the property belonging to the people killed... There is always someone making a profit! You will find them with their herds on the high grounds towards Hebron. But this is my advice: don't let anyone from Bethlehem see You speaking to them. You would suffer from it. We bear them because... because of the Herodian. Otherwise...'

'Oh! Hatred! Why hate?'

'Because it is just. They have done us harm.'

'They thought they were doing good.'

'But they did harm. Let them be harmed. We should have killed them as they had so many people killed through their stupidity. But we had become stupid ourselves and later... there was the Herodian.'

'So, even if he had not been there, after the first desire for revenge, which was still excusable, would you have killed them?'

'We would kill them even now, if we were not afraid of

their master.'

'Man, I tell you, do not hate. Do not wish evil things. Do not be anxious to do evil things. There is no fault here. But even if there was, forgive. Forgive in the name of God. Tell the other people of Bethlehem as well. When your hearts are free from hatred, the Messiah will come; you will know Him then, because He is alive. He already existed when the massacre took place. I am telling you. It was Satan's fault, not the fault of the shepherds and of the magicians that the massacre took place. The Messiah was born here for you, He came to bring the Light to the land of His fathers. The Son of a Virgin Mother of the line of David, in the ruins of the house of David, He granted a stream of Graces to the world, and a new life to mankind...'

'Go away! Get out of here! You are a follower of that false Messiah, Who could but be false, because He brought misfortune to us here in Bethlehem. You are defending Him, so...'

'Be silent, man. I am a Judaean and I have influential friends. I could make you feel sorry for your insult' bursts out Judas, getting hold of the peasant's garments, and shaking him in a fit of violent anger.

'No, No, out of here! I don't want trouble with the people of Bethlehem or with Rome or Herod. Go away, you cursed ones, if you don't want me to leave my mark on you... Out!'

'Let us go, Judas. Do not react. Let us leave him in his hatred. God will not enter where there is bitter hatred. Let us go.'

'Yes, we will go. But you will pay for it.'

'No, Judas, do not say that. They are blind... We shall

meet so many on My way.'

They go out and find Simon and John, who are outside, speaking to the woman, round the comer of the stable.

'Forgive my husband, Lord. I did not think I was going to cause so much trouble... Here, take these-' She gives Him some eggs- 'You will eat them tomorrow morning. They are newly laid. I have nothing else... Forgive us. Where will You sleep?'

'Do not worry. I know where to go. Go and peace be with you for your kindness. Goodbye.'

They walk a short distance, without speaking, then Judas bursts out: 'But You... Why not make him worship You? Why did You not crush that filthy swearer down in the mud? Down on the ground! Crushed because he showed no respect for You, the Messiah... Oh! That is what I would have done! Samaritans should be reduced to ashes by means of a miracle! It is the only thing that will shake them.'

'Oh! How many times will I hear that said! But if I should reduce to ashes for every sin against Me!... No, Judas. I have come to create, not to destroy.'

'Yes! And in the meantime they are destroying You.' Jesus does not reply.

Simon asks: 'Where are we going now, Master?'

'Come with Me, I know a place.'

'But if You have never been here after You left, how can You know?' asks Judas, still angry.

'I know. It is not a beautiful place. But I have been there before. It is not in Bethlehem... it is a little outside... Let us turn this way.'

Jesus is in front, followed by Simon, then Judas and John is last... In the silence, broken only by the rustling

of their sandals on the small grains of gravel of the path,
the sounds of sobbing can be heard.
'Who is crying?' asks Jesus turning round.

'It's John. He has been frightened.' answers Judas.
'No, I was not frightened. I had already laid my hand on
the knife under my belt... Then I remembered the words
You keep repeating: "Do not kill, forgive."'
'Why are you crying, then?' asks Judas.
'Because I suffer seeing that the world does not love
Jesus. They do not know Him, and they do not want to
know Him. Oh! It is such a pain! As if someone tore my
heart with burning thorns. As if I had seen someone
treading on my mother or spitting upon my father's
face... Even worse... As if I had seen Roman horses eating
in the Holy Ark and resting in the Holy of Holies.'
'Do not cry, My dear John. Say for this present time and
for endless times in future: "He was the Light and He
came to enlighten darkness – but darkness did not know
Him. He came to the world that had been made for Him,
but the world did not know Him. He came to His own
town, to His domain, but His own people did not accept
Him." Oh! Do not cry like that!'
'That does not happen in Galilee!' says John sighing.
'Well, not even in Judaea ' says Judas. 'Jerusalem is
the capital and three days ago it sang hosannas to You,
Messiah! You cannot judge from this place of coarse
peasants, shepherds and market gardeners. Also the
Galileans, mind you, are not all good. After all, where did
Judas, the false Messiah, come from? They said...'
'That is enough, Judas. There is no use in getting angry.
I am calm. Be calm, too. Judas, come here. I want to
speak to you. 'Judas goes near Him. 'Take this purse.

31

You will do the shopping for tomorrow.'
'And for the time being, where are we going to lodge?'
Jesus smiles, but does not reply.

It is dark and the vault of heaven is strewn with stars,
stars, stars as on a heavenly curtain, a canopy of living
gems spread over the hills of Bethlehem awash also in
the moonlight that turns everything white. Nightingales
are singing in the olives trees . Nearby, the silvery ribbon
of a brook bellows Oxen and bleatings of sheep. The air is
perfumed with the smell of the toasted hay of the mown
fields.

'But here!... There is nothing but ruins here! Where are
You taking us? The town is over there.'
'I know. Come. Follow the rivulet, behind Me. A few more
steps and then... then I will offer you the abode of the
King of Israel.'
Judas shrugs and becomes quiet.
A few more steps, then a heap of ruined houses: the
remains of houses... A cave between the clefts of a big
wall.
Jesus asks: 'Have You any tinder? Light it.'
Simon lights a small lamp which he has taken out of his
knapsack and gives it to Jesus.
'Come in 'says the Master lifting the lamp. 'Come in. This
is the nativity room of the King of Israel.'
'You must be joking, Master! This is a filthy den. Ah! I
am not going to stay here! I loathe it: it is damp, cold,
stinking, full of scorpions and perhaps also snakes...'
'And yet... My friends, here the night of the twenty-fifth
of Chislev, Feast of the Lights, Jesus Christ, was born of

the Virgin, the Immanuel, the Word of God made flesh, for the love of man: I Who am speaking to you. Also then, as now, the world was deaf to the voices of Heaven speaking to the hearts of men... and it rejected the Mother... and here... No, Judas, do not avert your eyes in disgust from those fluttering bats, from those green lizards, from those cobwebs, do not lift with disgust your beautiful embroidered mantle, lest it trail on the ground covered with animal excrement. Those bats are the grand daughters of the ones that were the first toys to be tossed before the eyes of the Child, for Whom the angels sang the "Gloria" heard by the shepherds, intoxicated only by an ecstatic joy, a true joy. The emerald green of those lizards was the first colour to strike My eyes, the first, after My Mother's white face and dress. Those cobwebs were the canopy of My royal cradle. This ground... oh! you may tread on it without disdain... It is littered with excrement... but it is sanctified by Her foot, the foot of the Holy, the Most Holy, Pure, Immaculate Mother of God, Who gave birth, because She was to give birth, because God, not man, told Her and covered Her with His shadow. She, the Faultless One, trod on it. You can tread on it, too. And may the purity diffused by Her, by the will of God, rise from the soles of your feet to your heart...'

Simon is on his knees. John goes straight to the manger and cries, leaning his head against it. Judas is terrified... he is overcome by emotion, and no longer worried about his beautiful mantle, he kneels on the ground, takes the edge of Jesus' tunic and kisses it and beats his breast saying: 'Oh! My good Master, have mercy on the blindness of Your servant! My pride vanishes... I see

33

You as You are. Not the king I was thinking of. But the
Eternal Prince, the Father of future centuries, the King of
peace. Have mercy, my Lord and my God, have mercy on
me!'

'Yes, you have all My mercy! Now we will sleep where the
Infant and the Virgin slept, over there where John has
taken the place of the adoring Mother, here where Simon
looks like My putative father. Or, if you prefer so, I will
speak to you of that night...'

'Oh! yes, Master, tell us of Your birth.'

'That it may be a bright pearl shining in our hearts. And
we may tell the whole world.'

'And we may venerate Your Virgin Mother, not only as
Your Mother, but also as... as the Virgin!'

Judas was the first to speak, then Simon and then John,
whose face smiles and cries, near the manger.

'Come and sit on the hay. Listen... 'and Jesus tells
them of the night of His birth.'... as the Mother was
near Her time to have Her Child, a decree was issued
by the imperial delegate Publius Sulpicius Quirinus
on instructions from Caesar Augustus, when Sentius
Saturninus was governor of Palestine. The decree stated
that a census had to be taken of all the people of the
empire. Those who were not slaves were to go to their
places of origin and register in the official rolls of the
empire. Joseph, the spouse of the Mother, was of the
line of David and the Mother was also of David's line. In
compliance with the decree, they left Nazareth and came
to Bethlehem, the cradle of the royal family. The weather
was severe...'

Jesus Goes To The Hotel In Bethlehem And Preaches From The Ruins Of Anne's House

It is early on a bright summer morning and little thin strips of pink cloud like brush strokes that look like strips of frayed gauze on a turquoise carpet.

Birds, exhilarated by the bright light, fill the air with the songs of Sparrows, blackbirds and redbreasts that whistle, chirp and brawl over a stem, a worm or a twig they want to take to their nests, to eat or on which to roost.

Swallows with rust coloured tops dart from the sky down to the little stream to wet their snow white breasts, refresh themselves in the water and catch a little fly still asleep on a little stem and then dart straight back up into the sky in a flash like a burnished blade, all the while, chattering joyfully.

Along the banks of the stream, two blue headed wagtails, dressed in pale ash- grey, walk gracefully like two little dames; holding up their long tails adorned with little velvet black spots. They stop to look with satisfaction at their beautiful reflections in the water before resuming their walk whilst a black bird, a real rogue of the wood, scoffs at them, whistling with its long beak.

In the thick foliage of a wild apple-tree growing all alone

by the ruins, a nightingale calls her mate insistently, only
becoming silent when she sees him coming with a long
caterpillar wriggling in the grip of his thin beak. Two city
pigeon escapees from a dove-cot that now dwell in the
freedom of a crevice in a ruined tower, give vent to their
effusions of love; the male cooing seductively for the
benefit of the modest female.

With His arms crossed, Jesus, looks at all the happy little
creatures and smiles.
'Are You already ready, Master? 'asks Simon, from
behind Him.
'Yes, I am. Are the others still sleeping? '
'Yes, they are. '
'They are young... I washed Myself in that stream... The
water is so cold that it clears the mind... '
'I'll go and wash now. '

While Simon, wearing only a short tunic, washes himself
and then puts his clothes on, Judas and John come out.
'Hail, Master, are we late? '
'No. It is only daybreak. But now be quick and let us go. '
The two get washed and put on their tunics and mantles.
Jesus, before setting off, picks some little flowers which
have grown between the crevices of two stones, and puts
them into a small wooden box that already contains other
items; 'I will take them to My Mother...'He explains. ' She
will love them... Let us go. '
'Where, Master? '
'To Bethlehem. '
'Again? I do not think the situation is a favourable one for
us... '

'It does not matter. Let us go. I want to show you where the Magi came and where I was. '

'In that case, listen. Excuse me, will You, Master? But let me do the talking. Let us do one thing. In Bethlehem and at the hotel, let me speak and ask questions. You Galileans are not awfully liked in Judaea, and much less here than anywhere else. Nay, let us do this: your clothes show that You and John are Galileans. It's too easy. And then... your hair! Why do you persist in wearing it so long? Simon and I will change mantles with you. Simon, give yours to John, I'll give mine to the Master. That's it! See? You already look a little more like Judaeans. Now take this. 'And he takes off the cloth covering his head: a yellow, brown, red, green striped length of material, like his mantle, held in position by a yellow cord, he places it on Jesus' head, adjusting it along His cheeks to hide His fair hair. John puts on the very dark green one of Simon. 'Oh! That's better now. I have a practical sense. '

'Yes, Judas, you have a practical sense. That is true. Watch, however, that it does not exceed the other sense. '

'Which one, Master? '

'The spiritual sense. '

'No! No! But in certain cases it pays to be more a politician than an ambassador. And listen... be good a little longer... it is for Your own good... Do not contradict me if I should say something... something... which is not true. '

'What do you mean? Why tell lies? I am the Truth and I want no lies in Me or around Me.'

'Oh! I will only tell half lies. I will say that we are all coming back from remote places, from Egypt for instance, and that we are seeking news of dear friends. I will say

that we are Judaeans coming back from exile. After all,
there is some truth in everything, and I will be speaking,
and... one lie more, one lie less... '

'But Judas! Why deceive? '

'Never mind, Master! The world lives on deceit. And at
times deceit is a necessity. Well: to make You happy, I
will only say that we are coming from far and that we are
Judaeans. Which is true for three out of four of us. And
you, John, please do not speak at all. You would give
yourself away. '

'I will be quiet. '

'Then... if everything works out all right... we shall say
the rest. But I do not believe it... I am shrewd, I grasp
things at once. '

'I see that, Judas. But I would prefer you to be simple. '

'It does not help much. In Your group, I will be the one in
charge of difficult missions. Let me carry on. 'Jesus is
reluctant. But He gives in.

They set out, walking first around the ruins and then
along a massive windowless wall from the other side of
which comes braying, mooing, neighing, bleating and the
queer cry of camels. They follow an angle in the wall and
emerge onto the square of Bethlehem with fountain at its
centre. The shape of the fountain is still slantwise as it
was on the night of the visit of the Magi but across the
street where the little house that on the same night had
been bathed in the silvery rays of the Star, there is now
only a large gap strewn with ruins, surmounted by the
little outside staircase and its landing.

Jesus looks and sighs.

The square is full of people around merchants of

foodstuffs, utensils, clothes and other items, all either
spread out on mats or in baskets on the ground, with
the merchants crouched in the centre of their... shops or
standing up, shouting and gesticulating with stingy
buyers.

'It's market day ' says Simon.
The main gate of the hotel where the Magi had stayed, is
wide open and a line of donkeys laden with goods is
coming out. Judas enters first and looks around
haughtily and seizes a dirty hustler in short sleeves, with
his short tunic reaching down to his knees. 'Hustler! 'he
shouts. 'The landlord! Quick! Be quick. I am not used to
being kept waiting for people. '
The boy runs away, dragging a broom behind him.
'But Judas! What manners! '
'Be quiet, Master. Leave me alone. It is important that
they consider us rich people coming from town. '
The landlord rushes in, and bows down repeatedly before
Judas, who looks impressive in Jesus' dark red mantle
worn on top of his sumptuous yellow tunic full of fringes.
'We have come from far, man. We are Judaeans of the
Asiatic communities. This gentleman, born in Bethlehem
and persecuted, is now looking for some dear friends. We
are with Him. We have come from Jerusalem, where we
worshipped the Most High in His House. Can You give us
some information? '
'My lord... your servant... will do everything for you. Give
me your orders. '
'We want some information on many... and particularly
on Anne, the woman whose house was opposite your
hotel. '

'Oh! poor woman! You will find her only in Abraham's bosom. And her children with her. '

'Is she dead? How? '

'Don't you know of Herod's massacre? The whole world talked about it and even Caesar called him "a pig who feeds on blood". Oh! What have I said? Don't report me! Are you really Judaen? '

'Here is the sign of my tribe. So? Speak up. '

'Anne was killed by Herod's soldiers, with all her children, except one daughter. '

'But why? She was so good? '

'Did you know her? '

'Yes, very well. 'Judas lies brazen-faced.

'She was killed because she gave hospitality to those who said they were the father and mother of the Messiah... Come here, into this room... Walls have ears and it is dangerous to talk about certain things. '

They go into a low dark room and sit on a low couch.

'Now... I had a wonderful nose. I am not a hotel keeper for nothing. I was born here, the son of sons of hotel keepers. Wiles are in my blood. And I did not take them. I could have found a hole for them. But... poor, unknown Galileans as they were... Oh! no! Hezekiah will not fall into the trap! And I felt... I felt they were different... that woman... Her eyes... something... no, no... She must have had a demon inside Her and She spoke to him. And She brought him... not to me... but to town. Anne was more innocent than a little lamb, and she gave them hospitality a few days later, when She already had the Child. They said He was the Messiah... Oh! the money I made during those days! The census was nothing like it! Many people came here who had nothing to do with the

census. They came even from the seaside, even from
Egypt to see... and it lasted for months! What a profit I
made! The last to come were three kings, three powerful
people, three magicians... I would not know! What a
train! An endless one!
They took all the stables and they paid in gold for so
much hay that could have lasted a month, and they went
away the following day, leaving it all here. And what gifts
they gave to the hustlers and the women!
And to me! Oh! I can only speak well of the Messiah,
whether He was a true or false one. He made me earn
bags of money. And I had no disasters. None of My family
died, because I had just got married. So...but the others!
'

'We would like to see the places of the slaughter. '
'The places? But every house was a place of slaughter.
There were people killed for miles round Bethlehem.
Come with me. '
They go up a staircase into a large terraced roof from
where they can see a lot of the countryside and the whole
of Bethlehem spread on the hills like an open fan.
'Can you see the ruined spots? Over there also the
houses were burnt down because the fathers defended
their children with their weapons. Can you see over
there, that thing like a well-covered with ivy? Those are
the remains of the synagogue. It was burnt down with
the arch synagogue who declared that it was indeed the
Messiah....burnt down by the survivors, driven wild
because of the slaughter of their children. We had trouble
for that after... And over there, and there, there... see
those sepulchres? The victims are buried there.. They
look like little sheep spread all over the green, as far as

the eye can see. All the innocents and their fathers and mothers... See that vat? Its water was red after the killers washed their weapons and hands in it. And the brook at the back here, did you see it? It was pink with the blood which had flowed into it from the sewers. And there, over there, in front of us. That is what is left of Anne's house.'
Jesus is crying.
'Did You know her well? '
Judas replies: 'She was like a sister for His Mother. Is that right, my friend? '
'Yes. ' says Jesus, simply.
'I understand ' remarks the hotel keeper who becomes pensive. Jesus bends forward to speak to Judas in a low voice.
'My friend would like to go on those ruins 'says Judas.
'Let Him go! They belong to everybody! '
They return downstairs, say goodbye and go out leaving the host who had been hoping to earn something, disappointed.
They cross the square and climb up the little staircase left standing over the ruins of Anne's house and onto the landing which is about two meters higher than the square.

'From here ' says Jesus, 'My Mother made Me wave My hand to the Three Wise Men and we left from here to go to Egypt. '
People look at the four men on the ruins and one asks: 'Are they relatives of Anne? '
'They are friends. '
'Don't do any harm to the poor dead woman...› one woman shouts ‹...don›t you do it, as her other friends did when she was alive, and then they ran away. '

Jesus is standing on the landing against the little wall
enclosing it with nothing behind Him but the unkempt
background of what was once Anne's kitchen garden and
field now laid waste and strewn with debris. The outline
of His figure is clearly cut against the sun shining behind
Him: it forms a halo around His golden hair, and makes
His snow white linen tunic look even whiter as it is the
only garment on Him, since His mantle has slipped off
His shoulders and is now lying at His feet like a multi-
coloured pedestal.

Jesus stretches out His arms but when Judas sees the
gesture he says: 'Don't speak! It isn't wise! '

But Jesus' powerful voice fills the square: 'Men of Judah!
Men of Bethlehem, listen! Women of the land sacred to
Rachel, listen! Listen to One Who descends from David,
and having suffered from persecutions, has become
worthy of speaking, and is speaking to you to give you
light and comfort. Listen. '

The people stop shouting, quarrelling and buying and
they gather together.

'He is a rabbi! '

'He certainly comes from Jerusalem. '

'Who is He? '

'What a handsome man! '

'And what a voice! '

'And His manners! '

'Of course, He is of David's House! '

'He is one of ours, then! '

'Let's listen to Him! '

The whole crowd is now gathered near the little staircase
that looks like a pulpit.

'In Genesis it is said: "I will make you enemies of each

other: you and the woman: She will crush your head and you will strike at Her heel." It is also said: "I will multiply your pains in childbearing... and the soil shall yield you brambles and thistles." That was the sentence against man, woman and the serpent. I have come from far to revere Rachel's tomb, and in the evening breeze, in the dew of the night, in the plaintive morning song of the nightingale,

I heard ancient Rachel›s sobs repeated, and they were repeated by the mouths of many mothers of Bethlehem, within their tombs or within their hearts. And I heard Jacob›s sorrow roar in the pain of the widowed husbands deprived of their wives, whom sorrow had killed... I cry with you... But listen, brethren of My land. Bethlehem; the blessed land, the least of the towns in Judah, but the greatest in the eyes of God and of mankind, roused Satan›s hatred because it was the cradle of the Saviour, as Micah says, destined to be the tabernacle on which the Glory of God, the Fire of God, His Incarnate Love was to rest.

"I will make you enemies of each other: you and the woman; She will crush your head and you will strike at Her heel." Which enmity is there greater than the one that aims at a mother's children, the very heart of a woman? And which heel is there stronger than the Saviour's Mother's? The revenge of Satan defeated was therefore a natural one: he did not strike at the heel, but at the hearts of mothers, because of the Mother.

Oh! Pains were multiplied when the children were lost after having giving birth to them! Oh! great was the trouble of being a childless father after sowing and toiling for the offspring! And yet, Bethlehem, rejoice! Your pure blood, the blood of the innocents has prepared a blazing purple way for the Messiah... '

At the mention of the Saviour and the Mother, the crowd became increasingly turbulent and is now showing clear signs of agitation.

'Be quiet, Master and let us go 'says Judas.

But Jesus goes on: '... for the Messiah that the Grace of the God-Father saved from tyrants to preserve Him for His people and its salvation and... '

The shrill voice of a woman yelling hysterically cuts through'... 'Five, five I gave birth to, and not one is now in my house. Poor me! '

The uproar begins.

Another woman, rolls over in the dust, she tears her dress and shows a breast maimed of its nipple, shouting: 'Here, here on this mamma they slaughtered my first-born son! The sword cut off his face and my nipple at the same time. Oh! my Ellis! '

'And what about me! What about me? There is my royal palace. Three tombs in one, watched over by the father: my husband and children together. There, there! If there is a Saviour, let Him give me back my children, my husband, let Him save me from despair, from Beelzebub He must save me. '

They all shout: 'Our children, our husbands, our fathers! Let Him give them back, if He exists! '

Jesus waves His arms imposing silence. 'Brethren of My land: I would like to give you back your children, in their flesh. But I tell you: be good, be resigned, forgive, hope, rejoice in hope and exult in one certainty: you will soon have your children, angels in Heaven, because the Messiah is about to open the gates of Heaven, and if you

are just, death will be a new Life and a new Love... '
'Ah! Are You the Messiah? In the name of God, tell us. '
Jesus lowers His arms in so sweet and kind a gesture as
though He were embracing them all, and He says:
'Yes, I am. '
'Go away! Go away! It's Your fault, then! ' There are
hisses and jeers and a stone cuts through the air heading
for the landing.
Judas reacting instinctively, jumps in front of Jesus,
standing on the low wall of the landing, with his mantle
opened wide and undaunted, he shields Jesus from the
stones. The stone catches Judas in the face, drawing
blood but he shouts to John and Simon: 'Take Jesus
away. Behind those trees. I'll follow. Go, in the name of
Heaven! 'And he shouts to the crowd: 'Mad dogs! I am of
the Temple and I will report you to the Temple and to
Rome. '
For a moment, the crowd is frightened. Then the shower
of stones resumes at once but fortunately, their aim is
off. And Judas, fearless, catches a stone thrown at him
and throws it back on the head of an old man who is
shouting like a magpie being plucked alive! Judas also
replies with offensive language to the curses of the crowd.

When the crowd tries to climb up to his pedestal, he
comes down from the little wall, quickly picks up an old
branch from the ground, and mercilessly swings it round
on backs, heads and hands. Some soldiers rush to the
spot and with their lances they make their way through
the crowd: 'Who are You? Why this brawl? '
'I am Judaean and I have been attacked by these
plebeians. A rabbi, well known to the priests, was with

me. He was speaking to these dogs. But they became wild and attacked us. '

'Who are You? '

'Judas of Kerioth, I was a man of the Temple. Now, I am a disciple of rabbi Jesus of Galilee and a friend of Simon the Pharisee, of Johanan the Sadducee, and of Joseph of Arimathaea, the Counsellor of the Sanhedrin, and finally, of Eleazar ben Anna, the Proconsul's great friend, and you can check. '

'I will. Where are you going? '

'I am going to Kerioth with my friend, then to Jerusalem.'

'Go. We will protect your back. '

Judas hands some coins to the soldier. It is illegal... but quite common, because the soldier takes them swiftly and cautiously, salutes and smiles. Judas jumps down from his platform and goes through the uncultivated field, skipping now and again until he reaches his companions.

'Are you seriously hurt? '

'No, it's nothing, Master! In any case, it's for You... But I gave them a licking as well. I must be covered with blood... '

'Yes, on your cheek. There is a rivulet here. '

John moistens a small piece of cloth and wipes Judas' cheek.

'I am sorry, Judas... But see... to tell them that we are Judaeans, according to your good practical sense... '

'They are beasts. I believe You are now convinced, Master. And I hope you will not insist... '

'Oh! no! Not because I am afraid. But because it is useless, just now. When they do not want us, we must not curse them, but withdraw praying for the poor, foolish people, who die of starvation and cannot see the Bread. Let us go along this out-of-the-way path, towards the shepherds, if we can find them. I think we will be able to get on to the toad to Hebron... '

'To have more stones thrown at us? '

'No. To say to them: "I am here." '

'What?... They will certainly beat us. They have been suffering for thirty years because of You. '

'We will see. '

And they disappear into a cool, shady, thick little wood.

Jesus And The Shepherds Elias, Levi And Joseph

The hills rise higher and higher and the woods grow thicker the further away from Bethlehem until they form a real chain of mountain. Jesus, climbing ahead, looks silently around as one anxious to find something. He listens, more to the voices of the woods than to the apostles' who are a few yards behind Him and are speaking to one another. Listening, He catches the ding-dong of a bell carried in the wind and smiles. Then turning round, He says;

'I hear the bells of sheep.'

'Where, Master?'

'I think near that hillock. But the wood prevents Me from seeing.'

Because of the heat, the apostles have taken off their mantles, rolled them up and are carrying them across their backs. Without another word, John also takes off his outer tunic and now, only with his short inner tunic on, he throws his arms around a tall smooth trunk of an ash tree and climbs up....until he can see.

'Yes, Master. There are many herds and three shepherds over there, behind that thicket.'

He comes back down and they proceed, sure of their way.

'Will it be them? '
'We shall ask, Simon, and if they are not, they will tell us
something... They know one another. '

After about a hundred yards, they emerge onto a wide
green pasture fully surrounded by gigantic very old trees
and many sheep grazing on the thick grass of the
undulating meadow. There are also three men, watching
over the sheep: One old with hair all turned white, a
second man of about thirty and the third of about forty
years of age.
'Be careful, Master. They are herdsmen... ' cautions
Judas, when he sees Jesus hastening His step.
But, without responding to Judas, Jesus hurries on, tall
and handsome in His white tunic and with the setting
sun in front of Him, He seems an angel.

'Peace be with you, My friends ' He greets when He
reaches the edge of the meadow.
The three men turn round, surprised. There is a silent
pause....and then the eldest man asks:
'Who are You? '
'One Who loves you. '
'You would be the first in so many years. Where are You
from? '
'From Galilee. '
'From Galilee? Oh! ' The man watches Him carefully....
and the other two draw nearer.
'From Galilee ' repeats the shepherd. And in a very low
voice, as one speaking to himself, he adds 'He came from
Galilee, too' aloud again, the shepherd asks again 'From
which town, my Lord? '

'From Nazareth. '

'Oh! Well, tell me. Has a Child ever come back to Nazareth, a Child with a woman whose name was Mary and a man called Joseph, a Child, Who was even more beautiful than His Mother, so beautiful that I have never seen a fairer flower on the slopes of Judah? A Child born in Bethlehem of Judah, at the time of the edict? A Child Who later fled, most fortunately for the world. A Child, oh! I would give my life just to hear whether He is alive... He must be a man by now. '

'Why do you say that His flight was a great fortune for the world? '

'Because He was the Saviour, the Messiah and Herod wanted Him dead. I was not there when He fled with His father and Mother. When I heard of the slaughter and I came back... because also I had children (he sobs), my Lord, and a wife... (he sobs), and I heard they had been killed (he sobs again), but I swear by the God of Abraham, I was more afraid for Him than for my own family – I heard He had fled and I could not even enquire; I could not even take away my own slaughtered creatures... They threw stones at me, as they do with lepers and unclean people, they treated me like a murderer... and I had to hide in the woods, and live like a wolf... until I found a master. Oh! it's no longer Anne... He is hard and cruel... If a sheep gets hurt, if a wolf preys on a lamb, he either beats me till I bleed or he takes my poor pay, and I have to work in the woods for other people, I must do something, to pay him back three times the value.

But it does not matter. I have always said to the Most High: "Let me see Your Messiah, at least let me know that

He is alive, and all the rest is nothing." My Lord, I have told You how the people in Bethlehem treated me, and how my master deals with me. I could have repaid them in their own coins, I could have wronged them, stealing, so that I would not suffer under my master. But I preferred to suffer, to forgive, to be honest, because the angels said: "Glory to God in the Highest Heaven and peace on earth to men of good will." '

'Is that what they said? '

'Yes, they did, my Lord, You must believe, at least You, Who are good. You must know and believe that the Messiah is born. No one would believe it any longer. But angels do not lie... and we were not drunk, as they said. This man here, was a boy then, and he was the first to see the angel. He drank but milk. Can milk make one drunk? The angels said: "Today, in the town of David the Saviour was born, He is Christ, the Lord. And here is a sign for you. You will find a Child wrapped in swaddling clothes lying in a manger." '

'Did they say exactly that? Did you not misunderstand them? Are you not mistaken, after such a long time? '

'Oh! no! Isn't it, Levi? In order not to forget, – we could not forget in any case, because they were heavenly words and were written in our hearts with a heavenly fire – every morning, every evening, when the sun rises, when the first star starts shining, we repeat them as a prayer, as a blessing, to have strength and comfort in His name and in His Mother's. '

'Ah! You said: "Christ"? '

'No, my Lord. We say: "Glory to God in the Highest Heaven and peace on earth to men of good will, through Jesus Christ Who was born of Mary in a stable in

Bethlehem and Who, wrapped in swaddling clothes, was in a manger, He Who is the Saviour of the world." '

'But, in short, whom are you looking for? '

'Jesus Christ, the Son of Mary, the Nazarene, the Saviour. '

'It is I. ' And Jesus is radiant as He reveals Himself to His persevering, faithful and patient lovers.

'You! Oh! Lord, Saviour, Our Jesus! 'The three men prostrate themselves on the ground and kiss Jesus' feet, crying with joy.

'Stand up. Get up. Elias and you, Levi and you, whose name I do not know. '

'Joseph, the son of Joseph. '

'These are My disciples, John, a Galilean, Simon and Judas, Judaeans. '

The shepherds are no longer prostrated on the ground, but kneeling, sitting back on their heels. And thus, they worship the Saviour with loving eyes and trembling lips, whilst their faces blanch and blush with joy. Jesus sits down on the grass.

'No, my Lord. You, King of Israel, must not sit on the grass. '

'Never mind, My dear friends. I am poor. A carpenter as far as the world is concerned. I am rich only in My love for the world, and in the love I get from good people. I have come to stay with you, to share the evening meal with you and sleep beside you on the hay, and to be comforted by you... '

'Oh! comfort! We are coarse and persecuted. '

'I am persecuted, too. But you give Me what I seek: love, faith and hope, a hope that will last for years and bear flowers. See? You waited for Me and you believed without

the least doubt, that I was the Messiah. And I have come
to you. '

'Oh! Yes! You have come. Now, even if I die, I will not be
upset that I hoped in vain. '

'No, Elias. You will live until Christ's triumph and after.
You saw My dawn, you must see My glory. And what
about the others? You were twelve: Elias, Levi, Samuel,
Jonah, Isaac, Tobias, Jonathan, Daniel, Simeon, John,
Joseph, Benjamin. My Mother always mentioned your
names to Me. Because you were My first friends. '

'Oh! ' The shepherds are more and more moved.

'Where are the others? '

'Old Samuel died of old age about twenty years ago.
Joseph was killed because he fought at the gate of the
enclosure to give time to his wife who had just become a
mother a few hours before, to escape with this man,
whom I took with me for the sake of my friend... also to
have children around me once again. I took Levi also with
me... He was persecuted. Benjamin is a shepherd on
Lebanon with Daniel. Simeon, John and Tobias, who now
wants to be called Matthew in memory of his father who
was also killed, are disciples of John.
Jonah works on the plain of Esdraelon for a Pharisee.
Isaac suffers very much from his back which is bent in
two. He lives in dire poverty, all by himself at Juttah. We
help him as much as we can, but we have all been badly
hit and our help is like dew drops on a fire. Jonathan is
now the servant of one of Herod's big men. '

'How did you, and particularly Jonathan, Jonah, Daniel
and Benjamin get such jobs? '

'I remembered Your relative Zacharias... Your Mother had
sent me to him. When we were in the mountain gorges in

Judaea, fugitives and cursed, I took them to him. He was good to us. He sheltered and fed us. And he found work for us. He did what he could. I had already taken all Anne's herd for the Herodian... and I remained with him... When the Baptist, grown into a man, began to preach, Simeon, John and Tobias went to him. '

'But now the Baptist is in jail. '

'Yes, and they are keeping watch near Machaerus, with a few sheep, to avoid arousing suspicion. They were given the sheep by a rich man, a disciple of Your relative John.'

'I would like to see them all. '

'Yes, My Lord. We will go and say to them: "Come, He is alive. He remembers us and loves us." '

'And He wants you to be His friends. '

'Yes, my Lord. '

'But we will go first to Isaac. And where are Samuel and Joseph buried? '

'Samuel in Hebron. He remained in Zacharias' service. Joseph... has no tomb. He was burned with the house. '

'He is no longer in the cruel fire, but in the flames of God's love and will soon be in His glory. I am telling you, and particularly you, Joseph, son of Joseph. Come here, that I may kiss you to thank your father. '

'And my children? '

'They are angels, Elias. Angels who will repeat the "Gloria" when the Saviour is crowned. '

'King? '

'No, Redeemer. Oh! What a procession of just people and saints! And in front there will be the white and purple phalanges of the martyrs! As soon as the gates of Limbo are opened, we shall ascend together to the eternal Kingdom. And then you will come and will find your

fathers, mothers and children in the Lord! Believe Me. '
'Yes, my Lord. '
'Call Me: Master. It is getting dark, the first evening star
is beginning to shine. Say your prayer before supper. '
'Not I. You say it, please. '
The disciples and shepherds remain kneeling whilst
Jesus stands up and with His arms outstretched, He
prays:
'Glory to God in the highest Heaven, and peace on earth
to men of good will who have deserved to see the Light
and serve it. The Saviour is among them. The Shepherd
of the royal line is with His herd. The morning Star has
risen. Rejoice, just people! Rejoice in the Lord. He Who
made the vaults of heaven and has strewn them with
stars, Who placed the seas at the boundaries of the land,
Who created winds and dew, and fixed the course of
seasons to give bread and wine to His children, He now
sends you a more Sublime food: the living Bread that
descends from Heaven, the Wine of the eternal Vine.
Come to Me, you who are the first of My worshippers.
Come to meet the Eternal Father in truth, to follow Him
in holiness and receive His eternal reward. '

The shepherds offer bread and new milk, and as there
are only three emptied marrows used for bowls, Jesus is
the first to eat, with Simon and Judas. Then John, to
whom Jesus hands His cup, with Levi and Joseph. Elias
is last.
The sheep have stopped grazing and are now gathered
together in a compact group perhaps waiting to be led to
their enclosure. The three shepherds lead the sheep into
the wood, to a rustic shed made with branches and

enclosed by ropes. Then busily, make beds of hay for
Jesus and His disciples, after which they light fires to
keep wild animals away.

Judas and John lie down and tired as they are, they are
soon fast asleep. Simon would like to keep Jesus
company he too soon falls asleep shortly afterwards,
sitting on the hay and leaning against a pole.

Jesus remains awake with the shepherds and they talk
about Joseph, Mary, the flight into Egypt, their return...
and after such questions about loving friendship, the
shepherds ask more noble questions like what they can
do to serve Jesus? How will they, poor, rough shepherds,
be able to do anything?

And Jesus teaches them and then explains: 'Now I am
going to go through Judaea. My disciples will keep in
touch with you all the time. Later I will let you come.
In the meantime, get together. Make sure that you are
all in touch with one another and that everyone knows
that I am here, in this world, as Master and Saviour. Let
everybody know, as best as you can. I will not promise
that you will be believed. I have been mocked at and
beaten. They will do the same to you.

But as you have been strong and just in your long
expectation, persist in being so, now that you are Mine.
Tomorrow, we will go towards Juttah. Then to Hebron.
Can you come? '

'Of course, we can. The roads belong to everybody and
the pastures to God. Only Bethlehem is forbidden by an
unfair hatred. The other villages know... but they jeer at
us, calling us "topers". Thus we will not be able to do very
much here. '

'I will employ you elsewhere. I will not abandon you. '

'For all our lifetimes? '

'For all My lifetime. '

'No, Master, I will die first. I am old. '

'Do you think so? I do not. One of the first faces I saw, Elias, was yours. It will also be one of the last. I will take with Me, impressed in My eyes, the image of your face deranged by sorrow for My death. But after, you will treasure in your heart the memory of the joy of a triumphal morning and will thus await death... Death: the everlasting meeting with Jesus, Whom you adored when He was a baby. Also then the angels will sing the Gloria: "for the man of good will." '

Jesus At Juttah With The Shepherd Isaac

It is early morning and the silvery tinkling of a little torrent fills the valley as its foamy waters flow southwards among the rocks, spreading its gay freshness out onto the little pastures along its banks but its moisture seems to climb up to the very green slopes of the hills, from the soil right through the bushes and shrubs of the brushwood and reaching right up to the top of the tall trees of the wood, mostly walnuts, giving the slope their beautiful varied shades of emerald green. Here and there in the wood are many green open spaces covered with thick grass that makes good healthy pasture for herds.

Jesus is walking down towards the torrent with His disciples and the three shepherds and now and again, He stops patiently to wait for a sheep that has been left behind or a shepherd who has had to run after a lamb that has gone astray- the Good Shepherd, He has provided Himself with a long branch to clear His path from blackberry, hawthorn and clematis branches that stick out in all directions and catch on garments, and the stick completes His pastoral figure.

'See? Juttah is up there. We will cross the torrent; there is a ford, which is very useful in summer, without having to use the bridge. It would have been quicker to come via Hebron. But You did not want that. '

'No. We will go to Hebron later. We must always go first to those who suffer. The dead do not suffer any longer when they have been just people. And Samuel was a just man. And if the dead need our prayers, it is not necessary to be near their bones to pray for them.

Bones? What are they? A proof of the power of God Who made man with dust. Nothing else.

Also animals have bones. But the skeletons of all animals are not so perfect as a man's skeleton. Only man, the king of creation, has an upright position, as a king over his subjects, and his face looks forwards and upwards without having to twist his neck; man looks upwards, towards the Abode of the Father. But they are still bones. Dust which will return to dust. The eternal Bounty has decided to assemble them again on the eternal Day to give an even greater joy to the blessed souls. Just imagine: not only the souls will be reunited and will love one another as and even more than they did on the earth, but they will rejoice also seeing one another with the same features they had on the earth: dear curly-haired children, like yours, Elias, fathers and mothers with loving hearts and faces like yours Levi and Joseph. Nay, in your case Joseph, it will be the day when at last you will see the faces for which you feel nostalgia. There are no more orphans, no widows among the just, up there...

Prayers for the dead can be said anywhere. It is the prayer of a soul for the soul of a relative to the Perfect

Spirit, Who is God, Who is everywhere. Oh! holy freedom of what is spiritual! There are no distances, no exile, no prisons, no tombs... There is nothing that can divide or restrict in painful impotence what is outside and above the chains of the flesh. You will go with your better part, towards your beloved ones. And they will come to you with their better part.

And the whole effusion of loving souls will rotate around the Eternal Fulcrum, around God: the Most Perfect Spirit, the Creator of everything that was, is and will be, Love that loves you and teaches you how to love... But here we are at the ford. I can see a row of stones emerging from the shallow water. '

'Yes, Master, it is that one there. At the time of floods, it is a roaring waterfall. Now there are seven streamlets flowing placidly between the six large stones of the ford. '

They reach the crossing where six large square-cut stones are laid about a foot apart from each other, across the torrent and the water, which reaches the stones in one large sparkling ribbon, is divided into seven minor ones that rush happily to re-join together again beyond the ford, to once again form one fresh stream that flows, babbling among the stones.

The shepherds watch the sheep cross, some walking on the stones, others preferring to cross in the stream that is only a foot deep and they drink the pure gurgling water.

Jesus crosses on the stones followed by His disciples and they resume walking on the other bank.

'You told me that You want to inform Isaac that You are here, but You do not want to go into the village? '

'Yes, that is what I want. '
'Well, we had better part. I will go to him, Levi and
Joseph will stay with the herd and with You. I'll go up
here. It will be quicker. '
And Elias starts to climb up the mountain side, towards
the white houses that are so bright up there in the
sunshine.
He reaches the first houses and goes along a tiny path
between houses and kitchen gardens and walks thus for
about ten meters and then turns into a wider road and
entering into the square.
The morning market is still on the square and
housewives and vendors are shouting under the shady
trees of the square.
Without stopping, Elias moves resolutely to the end of the
square and an attractive street begins, to a little house,
or rather, a room with the door wide open. Almost on its
threshold, in a little bed, lies an emaciated sick man
asking passers-by for alms in a plaintive voice. Elias
dashes in.
'Isaac... it's me. '
'You? I was not expecting you. You were here last month.'
'Isaac... Isaac... Do you know why I have come? '
'No, I don't... You are excited. What's happening? '
'I have seen Jesus of Nazareth, He is a man, now, a
rabbi. He came looking for me... and He wants to see us.
Oh! Isaac! Are you not well? '
Isaac, in fact, has fallen back as if he were dying. But he
comes round: 'No. The news... Where is He? What is He
like? Oh! If I could see Him! '
'He is down in the valley. He sent me to say to you exactly
this: "Come, Isaac, because I want to see you and bless

you." I'll call someone now to help me and I'll take you down. '

'Is that what He said? '

'Yes, it is. But what are you doing? '

'I'm going. '

Isaac throws away the blankets, he moves his paralyzed legs, he throws them off the straw mattress, he puts his feet on the floor, he stands up, still somewhat hesitating, and shaky. It all happens in an instant, under Elias' wide open eyes... who at last understands and begins to shout... A little woman looks in curiously. She sees the sick man stand up and cover himself with one of the blankets, since he has nothing else, and run away, shouting like a mad man.

'Let us go... this way, it will be quicker and we will not meet the crowd... Quick, Elias. 'They run through a little door of a kitchen garden in the back, they push the gate, made of dry branches, and once outside, they run along a narrow dirty path, then down a little road along kitchen gardens and finally through meadows and thickets, right down to the torrent.

'There is Jesus, over there 'says Elias, pointing Him out. 'The tall, handsome one, with fair hair, with a white tunic and red mantle... '

Isaac runs, he cuts through the grazing sheep, and with a cry of triumph, joy and adoration he prostrates himself at Jesus' feet.

'Stand up, Isaac. I have come. To bring you peace and blessings. Stand up, that I may see your face. '

But Isaac cannot stand up, overcome with excitement as he is and he remains prostrated, with his face on the ground, crying happily.

'You came at once. You did not worry whether you
could... '
'You told me to come... and I came. '
'He did not even close the door or pick up the alms,
Master. '
'It does not matter. The angels will watch his house. Are
you happy, Isaac? '
'Oh! My Lord! '
'Call Me Master. '
'Yes, my Lord, my Master. Even if you had not cured me,
I would have been happy to see You. How could I find so
much grace with You? '
'Because of your faith and patience, Isaac. I know how
much you suffered... '
'Nothing! nothing! It does not matter! I have found You.
You are alive. You are here. That's what matters. The
rest, all the rest is over. But, my Lord and my Master,
You are not going away any more, is that right? '
'Isaac, I have the whole of Israel to evangelize. I am
going... But if I cannot stay, you can always serve and
follow Me. Do you want to be My disciple, Isaac? '
'Oh! But I am not capable! '
'Can you avow Who I am? Avow it against jeers and
threats? And tell people that I called you and you came? '
'Even if You did not want, I would avow all that. I would
disobey You in that, Master. Forgive me for saying so. '
Jesus smiles. 'You can see then that you are capable of
becoming a disciple! '
'Oh! If that's all one has to do! I thought it was more
difficult, that we had to go to school with the rabbis to
learn how to serve You, the Rabbi of rabbis... and to go to
school at my age... 'The man in fact must be at least fifty

years old.

'You have done your schooling already, Isaac. '

'Me? No. '

'Yes, you have. Have you not continued to believe and love, to respect and bless God and your neighbour, not to be envious, not to wish what belongs to other people, and even what was your own and you no longer possessed, to speak only the truth, even if it should be harmful to you, not to associate with Satan committing sins? Have you not done all these things, in the last thirty years of misfortunes? '

'Yes, Master. '

'So you see, you have done your schooling. Go on doing so and, in addition, reveal to the world that I am in the world. There is nothing else to be done. '

'I have already preached You, Lord Jesus. I preached You to the children, who used to come, when I arrived lame in this village, begging for bread and doing some work, such as shearing and dairy work, and the children used to come round my bed, when I got worse and I was paralyzed from my waist downwards. I spoke of You to the children of many years ago, and to the children of present times, who are the sons of the previous ones... Children are good and they always believe... I told them of Your birth... of the angels... of the Star and the Wise Men... and of Your Mother... Oh! Tell me! Is She alive?'

'She is alive and She sends you Her regards. She always spoke of you all. '

'Oh! If I could see Her! '

'You will see Her. You will come to My house one day. Mary will greet you saying: "My friend". '

'Mary... yes, when you utter that name it is like filling

your mouth with honey... There is a woman in Juttah, she is a woman now, she had her fourth child not long ago, but once she was a little girl, one of my little friends... and she called her children: Mary and Joseph the first two, and as she dared not call the third one Jesus, she called him Immanuel, as a good omen for herself, her home and Israel. And she is now thinking of a name to give to her fourth child, born six days ago. Oh! When she hears that I am cured! And that You are here! Sarah is as good as homemade bread, and her husband Joachim is also so good. And their relatives? I owe them my life. They have always helped and sheltered me. '

'Let us go and ask them for hospitality during the hottest hours of the day and to bless them for their charity. '

'This way, Master. It is easier for the sheep and we will avoid the people, who are most certainly excited. The old woman, who saw me getting up, will have certainly told them. '

They follow the torrent, departing from it further south, to take a steep path along the mountainside shaped like the prow of a ship, moving in the opposite direction to the torrent now running along a beautiful uneven valley formed by the intersection of two mountain ranges.

A little dry-stone wall marks the boundaries of the estate that declines towards the valley. On the meadow, there are apple, fig and walnut trees, a kitchen garden with a well, the pergola and the flower beds and further along, a white house surrounded by green lawns, with a protruding wing that protects the staircase and forms a porch and loggia with a little dome on the highest part. There is a lot of shouting coming from the house.

Walking ahead, Isaac goes in and calls at the top of his voice: 'Mary, Joseph, Immanuel! Where are you? Come to Jesus. '

Three little ones: a girl of about five years old, and two little boys, about four and two years of age, run to Isaac, the youngest still somewhat uncertain on his legs. They are dumbfounded to see the... revived man. Then the little girl shouts: 'Isaac! Mummy! Isaac is here! Judith was right. '

A tall, buxom, brown, lovely woman emerges from a noisy room, most beautiful in her best dress: a snow-white linen dress, like a rich chemise falling in puckers down to her ankles. It is tied at her shapely waist with a multi-coloured striped shawl that covers her wonderful hips dropping in fringes down to her knees at the back. At the front, the chemise is tied under the filigree buckle and its ends hang loose.

A light veil decorated with rose branches on a beige background is pinned to her black plaits, like a tiny turban, and falls on to her neck in flowing folds and then onto her shoulders and breasts. It is held tight on her head by a small crown of medals tied together by a little chain. Heavy rings hang from her ears, and her tunic is held close to her neck by a silver necklace that passes through eyelets of her dress. And there are heavy silver bracelets on her arms.

'Isaac! What's this? Judith... I thought she had gone mad... But you are walking! What happened? '

'The Saviour! Oh! Sarah! He is here! He has come! '

'Who? Jesus of Nazareth? Where is He? '

'Over there! Behind the walnut-tree, and He wishes to know if you will receive Him! '

'Joachim! Mother! Come here, all of you! The Messiah is here! '

Women, men, boys, little ones run out shouting and yelling... but when they see Jesus, tall and stately, they lose heart and become petrified.

'Peace to this house and to you all. The peace and blessing of God. 'Jesus walks slowly, smiling, towards the group. 'My friends: will you give hospitality to the Wayfarer? 'and He smiles even more. His smile overcomes all fears. The husband takes heart: 'Come in, Messiah. We have loved You before meeting You. We shall love You more after meeting You. The house is celebrating today for three reasons: for You, for Isaac and for the circumcision of my third son. Bless him, Master. Woman, bring the baby! Come in, my Lord.'

They go into a room decorated for the feast. There are tables with foodstuffs, carpets and branches everywhere. Sarah comes back with a lovely new-born baby in her arms and presents him to Jesus.

'May God be always with him. What is his name? '

'No name yet. This is Mary, this is Joseph, this is Immanuel... but this one has no name yet... 'Jesus looks at the parents, who are close to each other, He smiles: 'Find a name, if he is to be circumcised today... 'They look at each other, they look at Him, they open their mouths and close them again without saying anything. Everyone is paying attention.

Jesus insists: 'The history of Israel has so many great, sweet, blessed names. The sweetest and most blessed ones have already been given. But perhaps there are still some left. '

The parents cry out together: 'Yours, Lord! 'and the

mother adds: 'But it is too holy... '

Jesus smiles and asks: 'When will he be circumcised? '

'We are waiting for the circumciser. '

'I will be present at the ceremony. And in the meantime I wish to thank you for what you have done for My Isaac. He no longer needs the help of good people. But good people still need God. You called your third son: God be with us. But you had God with you ever since you were charitable to My servant. May you be blessed. Your charity will be remembered in Heaven and on the earth. '

'Is Isaac going away now? Is he leaving us? '

'Does that upset you? But he must serve his Master. But he will come, and so will I. In the meantime, you will speak of the Messiah... There is so much to be said to convince the world! But here is the person you are expecting. '

A pompous personage comes in with a servant. There are greetings and low bows. 'Where is the child? 'he asks haughtily

'He is here. But greet the Messiah. He is here. '

'The Messiah! The one who cured Isaac? I heard about it. But.. We will talk about it after. I am in a great hurry. The child and his name. '

The people present are mortified by the man's manners. But Jesus smiles as if the impoliteness was not addressed to Him. He takes the baby, He touches his little forehead with His beautiful fingers, as if He wanted to consecrate him and says: 'His name is Jesai ' and then hands him back to his father, who goes into another room with the haughty man and other people. Jesus stays where He is until they return with the child, who is screaming desperately.

'Woman, give Me the child. He will not cry any longer ' He says to comfort the distressed mother. In fact, the child, once he is laid on Jesus' knees, becomes silent.

Jesus forms a group of His own, with the little ones around Him, and also the shepherds and disciples. The sheep that Elias has put in an enclosure are bleating outside. There is the noise of a party in the house. They bring sweets and drinks to Jesus. But Jesus hands them out to the little ones.

'Are You not drinking, Master? Will You not have anything. We are offering it warmly. '

'I know, Joachim, and I accept wholeheartedly. But let Me make the little ones happy first. They are My joy... '

'Pay no attention to that man, Master. '

'No, Isaac. I will pray that he may see the Light. John, take the two little boys to see the sheep. And you, Mary, come closer to Me and tell Me: Who am I? '

'You are Jesus, the Son of Mary of Nazareth, born in Bethlehem. Isaac saw You and he gave me the name of Your Mother, that I may be good. '

'To imitate Her, you must be as good as an angel of God, purer than a lily that blooms on top of a mountain, as pious as the holiest Levite. Will you be like that? '

'Yes, Jesus, I will. '

'Say: Master or Lord, little girl. '

'Let her call Me with My name, Judas. Only when it is uttered by innocent lips, it does not lose the sound that it has on My Mother's lips. Everybody, throughout future centuries, will mention that name, some because of an interest or other, some to curse it. Only innocent people, without any interest and any hatred, will pronounce it with the same love as this little girl and My Mother.

73

Also sinners will invoke Me, because they need mercy. But My Mother and the little ones! Why do you call Me Jesus? ' He asks, caressing the little girl.

'Because I love You... as I love my father, mother and my little brothers ' she replies, embracing Jesus' knees, and smiling with her head turned upwards. And Jesus bends down and kisses her.

Jesus At Hebron. Zacharias' House. Aglae.

'At what time will we be arriving?' asks Jesus, walking at the centre of the group behind the sheep, grazing on the grass on the banks.

'At about the third hour. It's almost ten miles ' replies Elias.

'Are we going to Kerioth afterwards?' asks Judas.

'Yes, we will go there.'

'Was it not quicker to go to Kerioth from Juttah? It cannot be a great distance. Is that correct, shepherd? '

'About two miles longer, more or less.'

'This way, we will be doing over twenty for nothing.'

'Judas, why are you so worried? '

'I am not worried, Master. But You promised You would come to my house.'

'And I will. I always keep My promises.'

'I sent word to my mother... and after all, You said so Yourself, one can be near the dead also with one's soul.'

'I did. But just think, Judas: you have not yet suffered because of Me. These people have been suffering for thirty years, and they have never betrayed, not even My memory. They did not know whether I was dead or alive... and yet they remained faithful. They remembered

Me as a newly-born baby, an infant with nothing but tears and the need of milk... and they have always worshipped Me as God. Because of Me they have been beaten, cursed and persecuted as if they were the disgrace of Judaea, and yet their faith has never faltered. Neither did it wither under blows, on the contrary it took deeper roots and became stronger.'

'By the way. For some days I have been anxious to ask You a question. These people are Your friends and the friends of God, are they not? The angels blessed them with the peace of Heaven, did they not? They have been faithful against all temptations, have they not? Would You explain to me, then, why they are unhappy? And what about Anne? She was killed because she loved You...'

'Are you therefore deducing that to be loved by Me and to love Me brings bad luck?'

'No... but...'

'But you are. I am sorry to see you so closed to the Light and so open to human things. No, never mind John, and you too, Simon. I prefer him to speak. I never reproach. I only want you to open your souls to Me that I may enlighten them.

Come here, Judas, listen. You are basing yourself on an opinion that is common to many people of our times and will be common to many in future. I said: an opinion. I should say: an error. But since you do not do so out of malice, but out of ignorance of the truth, it is not an error, it is only an incorrect opinion like a child's. And you are like children, My poor men. And I am here, as a Master, to make adults of you, capable of telling the truth from the false, good from bad and what is better from what is good. Listen to Me, therefore.

What is life? It is a period of pause, I would say the limbo of Limbo, that the God Father grants you as trial to ascertain whether you are good or bad children, after which He will allot, according to your deeds, a future life without pauses or trials. Now tell Me: would it be fair if a man, simply because he has been granted the rare gift of being in the position of serving God in a special way, had also an everlasting wealth throughout his life? Do you not think that he has already been granted a great deal and may therefore consider himself happy, even if human things are against him? Would it not be unfair if he, who already has the light of divine revelation in his heart and the smile of a clear conscience, should also have worldly honours and wealth? And would it not also be unwise?'

'Master, I would also say that he would be a desecrator. Why put human joys where You already are? When one has You – and they had You, they are the only rich people in Israel because they have had You for thirty years – one should have nothing else. We do not put human things on the Propitiatory... and the consecrated vase is used only for sacred uses. And these people are consecrated since the day they saw Your smile... and nothing but You is to enter their hearts, which possess You. I wish I was like them! ' says Simon.

'But you wasted no time, immediately after you saw the Master and were cured, in getting back your property ' Judas replies sarcastically.

'That is true. I said I would and I did. But do you know why? How can you judge if you do not know the whole situation? My representative was given precise instructions. Now that Simon Zealot has been cured

– and his enemies can no longer harm him, neither can they persecute him because he belongs only to Jesus and to no sect: he has Jesus and nothing else – Simon can dispose of his wealth which an honest and faithful servant kept for him. And I, being the owner for a further short time, gave instructions that the estate should be reorganised, so that I would get more money when selling it and I would be able to say... no, I am not telling what.'

'The angels tell, Simon and they are writing it in the eternal book ' says Jesus.

Simon looks at Jesus. Their eyes meet: Simon's express surprise, Jesus' blessing approval.

'As usual. I am wrong.'

'No, Judas. You have a practical sense, you said so yourself. '

'Oh! but with Jesus!... Also Simon Peter was full of practical sense, now instead!... You, too, Judas, will become like him. You have only been with the Master a short time, we have been longer with Him and we are already better ' says John who is always kind and conciliatory.

'He did not want me. Otherwise I would have been His since Passover. ' says Judas plaintively.

Jesus puts an end to the argument by asking Levi: 'Have you ever been to Galilee? '

'Yes, my Lord. '

'You will come with Me to take Me to Jonah. Do you know him? '

'Yes, I do. We always met at Passover. I used to go and see him then.'

Joseph, mortified, lowers his head. Jesus notices and says: 'You cannot both come. Elias would be left alone with the sheep. But you will come with Me as far as the Jericho pass where we will part for some time. I will tell you afterwards what you have to do. '

'What about us? Will we not do anything? '

'Yes, you will, Judas, you will.'

'There are some houses over there ' says John, walking a few steps in front of the others.

'It's Hebron. Between two rivers with its crest. See, Master? That house there, amidst all the green, a little higher up than the others? That's Zacharias' house.'

'Let us quicken our paces.'

The sheep's little hooves click like castanets on the uneven stones of the roughly paved road as they quicken their pace, rapidly cover the last stretch of the road and enter the village.

People stare at the group of men, so different by look, age and garments amongst the white sheep. They reach the house.

'Oh! It's different! There was a gate here! ' says Elias. Now, instead, there is a metal door that prevents one from seeing, and also the enclosure wall is higher than a man and thus nothing can be seen inside.

'Perhaps it will be open at the back. 'They go round a large rectangular wall but find it is the same height all round.

'The wall was built not long ago ' remarks John, examining it. 'There is not a scratch on it and there is still lime rubble on the ground. '

'I cannot even see the sepulchre... It was near the wood. Now the wood is outside the wall and... and it seems to belong to everybody. They are gathering firewood in it. 'Elias is puzzled.

A small but strong looking man, an old woodcutter, who
is watching the group, stops sawing a trunk lying on the
ground and goes towards the group. 'Whom are you
looking for?'

'We wanted to go in to pray on Zacharias' tomb '.

'There is no tomb any longer. Don't you know? Who are
you? '

'I am a friend of Samuel, the shepherd. This... '

'It is not necessary, Elias ' says Jesus and Elias keeps
quiet.

'Ah! Samuel!... I see! But since John, Zacharias' son, was
put into prison, the house is no longer his. And it is a
misfortune because all the profit of his property was
given to the poor people in Hebron. One morning a man
came from Herod's court, he threw Jowehel out, he
affixed seals, then he came back with bricklayers and
they started raising the wall... The sepulchre was over
there in the corner. He did not want it... and one morning
we found it all spoiled and half destroyed... the poor
bones all scattered... We put them together again as well
as we could... They are now in a sarcophagus... And in
the house of the priest, Zacharias, that filthy man keeps
his lovers. Now there is a mime from Rome. That is why
he raised the wall. He does not want people to see... The
house of the priest a brothel! The house of the miracle
and of the Precursor! For it is certainly him, if he is not
the Messiah. And how much trouble we had because of
the Baptist! But he is our great man! He is really great!
Even when he was born there was a miracle. Elizabeth
was as old as a withered thistle but she became as
fruitful as an apple in Adar* and that was the first
miracle. Then a cousin of hers came and She was a holy

woman and She served her and loosened the priest›s
tongue. Her name was Mary. I remember Her although
we saw Her very rarely. How it happened I don›t know.
They say that to make Elizabeth happy, She made
Zacharias put his mute mouth against Her pregnant
bosom or that She put Her fingers into his mouth. I don›t
know. It is a fact that after nine months› silence,
Zacharias spoke praising the Lord and saying that there
was a Messiah. He did not explain more. But my wife was
there that day and she assured me that Zacharias,
praising the Lord, said that his son would precede Him.
Now I say: it is not what people believe. John is the
Messiah and he goes before the Lord, as Abraham went
before God. That›s what it is. Am I not right? '

*Adar is the sixth month in the Jewish calendar falling
between February and March.

'You are right with regard to the spirit of the Baptist, who
always proceeds before God. But you are not right with
regard to the Messiah'
'Well, the woman who said that She was the Mother of
the Son of God – Samuel said so – was it not true that
She was? Is She still living? '
'Yes, She was. The Messiah was born, preceded by him
who raised his voice in the desert, as the Prophet said.'
'You are the first to say so. John, the last time that
Jowehel took him a sheepskin, which he did every year at
the beginning of winter, although he was questioned
about the Messiah, did not say: "The Messiah is here."
When he will say so…'
'Man, I was a disciple of John and I heard him say: "Here

81

is the Lamb of God" pointing to... ' says John.

'No, no. He is the Lamb. A true Lamb who grew up by himself, almost without the need of a father and mother. As soon as he became a son of the Law, he lived isolated in the mountain caves overlooking the desert, and he grew up there conversing with God. Elizabeth and Zacharias died, and he did not come. God only was his father and mother. There is no holy man greater than he is. You can ask everyone in Hebron. Samuel used to say so, but the people in Bethlehem must have been right. John is the holy man of God. '

'If someone said to you: "I am the Messiah", what would you say? ' asks Jesus.

'I would call him a "blasphemer" and I would drive him away, throwing stones at him. '

'And if he worked a miracle to prove that he was the Messiah? '

'I would say that he was "possessed". The Messiah will come when John reveals himself in his true nature. The very hatred of Herod is the proof. Cunning as he is, he knows that John is the Messiah.'

'He was not born in Bethlehem.'

'But when he is freed, after announcing by himself his impending coming, he will reveal himself in Bethlehem. Also Bethlehem is waiting for that. Whilst... Oh! Go, if you have plenty of guts, and talk to the Bethlehemites of another Messiah... and you will see...'

'Have you a synagogue?'

'Yes, about two hundred steps straight ahead. You cannot go wrong. Near it there is the sarcophagus with the violated remains.'

'Goodbye, may God enlighten you.'

They go away, make a right turn on to the front of the house and find, at its door, a beautiful young impudently dressed woman. 'My Lord, do you wish to come into the house? Come in.'

Jesus stares at her as severe as a judge but does not speak. But Judas does, supported by all the others.

'Go back in, shameless woman! Do not desecrate us with your breath, ravenous bitch.'

The woman blushes, bows her head and is about to disappear abashed and scoffed at by urchins and passers-by.

'Who is so pure as to say: "I have never desired the apple offered by Eve?" ' Jesus asks, severely. 'Show Me him and I will call him a holy man. Nobody? Well, then, if not out of disgust, but out of weakness, you feel unable to go near this woman, you may withdraw. I will not force weaklings into unequal struggles. Woman, I would like to come in. This house belonged to a relative of Mine and is dear to Me.'

'Come in, my Lord, if You do not loathe me.'

'Leave the door open, that the world may see and may not tattle...'

Jesus enters, serious and solemn.

The woman, subdued, bows down before Him and dares not move. But the quips of the people cut her to the quick so she runs away to the end of the garden, while Jesus goes as far as the foot of the staircase. He looks in through the half open doors but does not enter. Then He goes to the place where the sepulchre once was, where there is now a small pagan temple.

'The bones of the just, also when dry and scattered, ooze a purifying balm and spread seed of eternal life. Peace to

the dead who lived doing good! Peace to the pure who are sleeping in the Lord! Peace to those who suffered, but knew no vice! Peace to the real great ones of the world and of Heaven! Peace! '

Walking along the protective hedge, the woman has reached Jesus.

'My Lord! '

'Woman.'

'Your Name, my Lord.'

'Jesus. '

'I never heard it. I am Roman: a mime and dancer. I am an expert only in lust. What is the meaning of Your name? My name is Aglae and... and it means: vice.'

'Mine means: Saviour.'

'How do You save? And whom?'

'Those who are anxious to be saved. I save by teaching to be pure, to prefer sorrows to honours, to desire good at all costs.' Jesus speaks without bitterness, without even turning towards the woman.

'I am lost...'

'I am the One seeking who is lost.'

'I am dead.'

'I am the One who gives Life.'

'I am filth and falsehood.'

'I am Purity and Truth.'

'You are also Bounty, You do not look at me. You do not touch me, You do not tread on me. Have mercy on me...'

'First, you must have mercy on yourself. On your soul.'

'What is the soul?'

'It is what makes a god of man and not an animal. Vice and sin kill it and once it is killed, man becomes a repulsive animal.'

'Will it be possible for me to see You again?'

'Who looks for Me, finds Me.'

'Where do You live?'

'Where hearts need doctors and medicines to become honest again.'

'In that case... I will not see You again... I live where no doctor, medicine or honesty is wanted.'

'Nothing prevents you from coming to where I am. My name will be shouted in the streets and will reach you. Goodbye.'

'Goodbye, my Lord. Allow me to call You "Jesus". Oh! Not out of familiarity!

... But that a little of salvation may come to me. I am Aglae, remember me.'

'I will. Goodbye.'

The woman stays at the end of the garden whilst Jesus comes out of it looking severe and a servant closes the door. He looks at everybody, sees perplexity in His disciples and hears jeers from the Hebronites.

Walking straight along the road, Jesus knocks at the synagogue and a resentful man looks out.

'The synagogue is forbidden, in this holy place, to those who deal with prostitutes.

Go away.' says the man, not even giving Jesus time to speak.

Without a reply, Jesus turns away and continues walking along the road, followed by His disciples.

Outside Hebron, they begin to speak.

'You asked for trouble, Master ' says Judas. 'A prostitute, of all people! '

'Judas, I solemnly tell you that she will surpass you. And

now, since you are reproaching Me, what do you say of
the Judaeans? In the most holy places in Judaea we have
been scoffed at and driven away... That is the truth. The
day will come when Samaria and the Gentiles will
worship the true God, and the people of the Lord will be
soiled with blood and a crime... a crime in comparison
with which the sins of prostitutes who sell their bodies
and their souls, will be a very small thing. I was not able
to pray on the tomb of My cousins and of the just
Samuel. It does not matter. Rest, holy bones, rejoice,
souls, that dwelt in them. The first resurrection is near.
Then the day will come when you will be shown to the
angels as the souls of the servants of the Lord.'

At The Jordan Ford. Meeting With The Shepherds John, Matthias And Simeon

There are lines of little donkeys and people coming and going along the beaten road that runs along the green banks of the Jordan. Also on the river bank, are three men guarding a few sheep in the pasture.
Joseph is waiting on the road, looking up and down.
In the distance, at the junction of the river path with the main road, Jesus appears with His three disciples.
Josephs calls out to the shepherds who driving the sheep along the grassy bank, walk fast towards Jesus.
'I haven't got the courage... What shall I say to greet Him? '
'Oh! He is so good! Say: "Peace be with You." He always says that. '
'Yes, He... but we... '
'And what about me? I am not even one of His first worshippers and He is so fond of me... oh! so fond! '
'Which one is it? '
'The tallest One, with fair hair.'
'Matthias, will we tell Him of the Baptist?'
'Of course we will! '
'Will He not think that we preferred the Baptist to Him? '
'No, Simeon. If He is the Messiah, He can see into the

hearts of men and in ours He will see that in the Baptist we were still looking for Him.'

'Yes, you are right.'

With the two groups now only a few yards apart, the shepherds can see Jesus smiling at them with His indescribable smile and Joseph hastens his step. The sheep, urged by the herdsmen, also begin to run.

'Peace be with you ' says Jesus raising His arms in a wide embrace. 'Peace to you, Simeon, John and Matthias, faithful to Me, and faithful to John the Prophet!...' He adds specifically to each of the shepherds who are now down on their knees. '...Peace to you, Joseph ' and He kisses him on his cheeks. 'Come, My friends. Under these trees on the exposed river-bed and let us talk. '

They go down to the exposed riverbed where Jesus sits on a large protruding root and the others on the ground. Jesus smiles and looks at them intently, one by one: 'Let Me become familiar with your faces. Your souls are already known to Me, souls that seek and love what is good contrary to all worldly yearnings. Isaac, Elias and Levi send you their regards and there are other greetings from My Mother. Have You any news of the Baptist? '

The men, so far gagged by embarrassment, take heart and find words at last: 'He is still in jail. Our hearts tremble for him because he is in the hands of a cruel man who is dominated by an infernal creature and is surrounded by a corrupt court. We love him... You know that we love him and that he deserves our love. After you left Bethlehem, we were persecuted by men... but we were distressed and disheartened because we had lost You, rather than by their hatred, and we were like trees

uprooted by the wind. Then, after years of suffering, like
a man whose eyelashes have been stitched struggles to
see the sun, but cannot, also because he is closed in a
prison but feels the warmth of the sun on his body, we
felt that the Baptist was the man of God foreseen by the
Prophets to prepare the way to His Christ and we went to
him. We said: "If the Baptist precedes Him, if we go to the
Baptist, we will find Him." Because, my Lord, it was You
we were looking for. '
'I know. And you found Me. And now I am with you. '
'Joseph told us that You came to the Baptist. But we
were not there that day. Perhaps he had sent us
somewhere. We serve him in spiritual matters, when he
asked us, with so much love. And we listened to him with
love, although he was so severe, because he was not You
– the Word – but he always spoke words of God.'
'I know. And do you know this man? ' Jesus asks,
pointing to John.
'We saw him with the other Galileans in the crowds which
were most faithful to the Baptist. And, if we are not
mistaken, you are the one whose name is John, and of
whom he used to say to us, his closest disciples: "Here: I
am the first, he is the last. And then: he will be the first
and I the last." But we never understood what he meant.'
Jesus turns to John on His left and He draws him
against His heart and with a most kind smile He
explains: 'He meant that he was the first to say: "Here is
the Lamb" and that John here will be the last of the
friends of the Son of man to speak of the Lamb to the
crowds; but that in the heart of the Lamb, John is the
first, because he is dearer than any other man to the
Lamb. That is what he meant. But when you see the

Baptist – You will see him again, and you will serve him again until the predetermined hour – tell him that he is not the last in Christ's heart. Not so much because of the blood, as on account of his holiness, he is loved as much as John. And remember that. If the saint in his humility proclaims himself "last", the Word of God proclaims him equal to the disciple who is dear to Me.. Tell him that I love this disciple because he has the same name and because I find in him the signs of the Baptist, who prepares the souls for Christ.'

'We will tell him... But will we see him again? '

'Yes, you will. '

'Yes, Herod dare not kill him for fear of the people and at his court, which is full of greed and corruption, it would be easy to free him if we had a lot of money. But, although there is quite a lot – because friends have given a lot – there is still a lot missing. And we are afraid we will not be in time... and he may be killed. '

'How much do you think you need for the ransom? '

'Not for his ransom, Lord. Herodias hates him too much and she has too much control of Herod to allow the possibility of a ransom. But I think that all the greedy people of the kingdom have gathered at Machaerus. Everybody is anxious to have a good time and stand out; from the ministers down to the servants. And to do that, they need money... We have also found who would let the Baptist out for a large sum of money. Perhaps also Herod would prefer that... because he is afraid. Not for any other reason. He is afraid of the people and afraid of his wife. In that way, he could please the people and his wife could not accuse him of disappointing her.'

'And how much does that person want? '

'Twenty silver talents. But we have only twelve and a
half.'

'Judas, you said that those jewels are beautiful. '

'Yes, beautiful and valuable.'

'How much will they be worth? I think you are an expert.'

'Yes, I am a good judge. Why do You want to know how
much they are worth, Master? Do You want to sell them?
Why? '

'Perhaps... Tell Me: how much will they be worth? '

'At least six talents, if they are sold well. '

'Are you sure? '

'Yes, Master. The necklace by itself, so big and heavy, of
the purest gold, is worth at least three talents. I have
examined it carefully. And also the bracelets... I don't
know how Aglae's thin wrists could hold them. '

'They were her shackles, Judas.'

'That's true, Master... But so many would like to have
such beautiful shackles!'

'Do you think so? Who? '

'Well... many people! '

'Yes, many who are human beings only by name... And
do you know a possible buyer? '

'So, do You want to sell them? And is it for the Baptist?
But look, it's cursed gold! '

'Oh! Human inconsistency! You have just said with
evident desire, that many people would love to have that
gold, and then you say it is cursed?! Judas, Judas!... It is
cursed, indeed. But she said: "It will be sanctified if it is
used for poor and holy people" and that is why she gave
it, that who benefits by it, may pray for her poor soul that
like the embryo of a future butterfly swells in the seed of
her heart. Who is holier and poorer than the Baptist? He

is equal to Elijah in his mission but greater than Elijah in holiness. He is poorer than I am. I have a Mother and a home... And when one has such things, and pure and holy as I have, one is never forlorn. He no longer has a home, and he has not got even the tomb of his mother. Everything has been violated and desecrated by human iniquity. So who is the buyer? '

'There is one in Jericho and there are many in Jerusalem. But the one in Jericho!!! He is a shrewd Levantine gold-beater, a loan shark, a middleman, a pander, he is certainly a thief. Probably a killer. He is definitely persecuted by Rome. He has changed his name to Isaac, to pass for a Hebrew... But his real name is Diomedes. I know him very well... '

'Yes, we see that!... 'intervenes Simon Zealot, who speaks little, but notices everything.'...How come you know him so well? '

'Well... you know... In order to please certain mighty friends. I went to see him... and did some business... You know... we of the Temple... '

'I know... you do all sorts of jobs ' concludes Simon with cold irony. Judas flares up, but keeps silent.

'Will he buy? ' asks Jesus.

'I think so. He has plenty money. Of course, one must be skilful in selling because the Greek is shrewd and if he realizes he is dealing with an honest person, with a nestling dove, he plucks him mercilessly. But if he has to deal with a vulture like himself...'

'You ought to go, Judas. You are the right man. You are as sly as a fox and as predatory as a vulture. Oh! Forgive me, Master. I spoke before You! ' says Simon Zealot again.

'I am of the same opinion, and I will therefore tell Judas
to go. John, you will go with him. We will meet again at
sunset and the meeting place will be the market square.
Go. And do your best.'

Judas gets up at once and John turns his imploring
chastened puppy's eyes on Jesus, who, speaking to the
shepherds, does not notice so John sets out behind
Judas.

'I would like to see you happy ' says Jesus.

'You will always make us happy, Master. May God bless
You for it. Is that man a friend of Yours? '

'Yes, he is. Do you think he should not be? '

The shepherd John lowers his head, and keeps silent but
Simon speaks: 'Only who is good, can see. I am not good,
and therefore I do not see what Bounty sees. I see the
exterior. Who is good penetrates also into the interior.
You, John, see as I do. But the Master is good... and
sees... '

'What do you see in Judas, Simon? I want you to tell Me.'

'Well, when I look at him, I think of certain mysterious
places that look like dens of wild beasts and malaria
infested ponds. One can only see a huge tangle and,
frightened, one keeps clear... Instead... behind it there
are turtle-doves and nightingales and the soil is rich in
healthy waters and good herbs. I want to believe that
Judas is like that... I think he must be, because You
chose him. And You know... '

'Yes, I know... There are many flaws in the heart of that
man... But he has some good points. You saw that
yourself in Bethlehem and in Kerioth. And his good
points which are humanly good are to be raised to a
spiritual goodness. Judas will then be as you would like

95

him to be. He is young... '

'Also John is young... '

'And in your heart, you conclude that he is better. But John is John! Love poor Judas, Simon, I beg you.. If you love him... he will appear to be better. '

'I try to love him for Your sake. But he breaks all my efforts as though they were water canes... But, Master, there is only one law for me: to do what You want. I will, therefore, love Judas although something within me shouts out to me against him'

'What, Simon? '

'I do not know exactly what it is: something that resembles the cry of the night watchman... and says to me: "Do not sleep! Watch!" I do not know. That something has no name. But it is here... in me, against him. '

'Forget about it, Simon. Do not trouble to give it a definition. It is better not to know certain truths... and you might be mistaken. Leave it to your Master. Give Me your love and you can be sure that it makes Me happy... '

Jesus And Isaac Near Doco. Departure Towards Esdraelon

'And I tell You, Master, that humble people are better...'
Isaac reports to Jesus. '...the ones I spoke to either
laughed at me or ignored me. Oh! The little ones at
Juttah! '
They are seated in a group on the grass by the riverbank
and Judas interrupts Isaac, exceptionally calling the
shepherd by name;
'Isaac, I am of your opinion. We waste our time and lose
our faith dealing with them. I am giving it up.'
'I will not but it makes me suffer. I will give up only if the
Master tells me. For years I have been accustomed to
suffering out of loyalty to the truth. I could not tell lies to
get into the good graces of the mighty ones. And do you
know how many times they came to make fun of me in
the room where I was ill, promising help – oh! they were
certainly false promises – if I would say that I had lied
and that You, Jesus, were not the New-Born Saviour?!
But I could not lie. If I had lied I would have denied my
own joy, I would have killed my only hope, I would have
rejected You, my Lord! Reject You! In my dark misery in
my dreary illness there was always a sky strewn with
stars above me: the face of my mother who was the only

joy of my orphan life, the face of a bride who was never mine and whom I continued to love even after her death. These were the two minor stars. And the two major stars, like two most pure moons: Joseph and Mary smiling at the New-Born Baby and at us poor shepherds, and Your bright, innocent, kind, holy, holy, holy face, in the centre of the sky of my heart. I could not reject that sky of mine! I did not want to deprive myself of its light as there is no other so pure. I would have rather rejected my own life or I would have lived in torture rather than reject You, My blessed remembrance, my New-Born Jesus! '

Jesus lays His hand on Isaac's shoulder and smiles.

'So you insist? ' persists Judas

'I do. Today, tomorrow and the day after again. Someone will come.'

'How long will the work last? '

'I don't know. But believe me. It is enough not to look either ahead or behind and do things day by day. And in the evening, if we have worked with profit, we say: "Thank You, my God". If without profit, just say: "I hope in Your help for tomorrow." '

'You are wise. '

'I don't even know what it means. But I do in my mission what I did during my sickness. Thirty years of infirmity is no trifling matter! '

'Ehi! I believe that. I was not yet born and you were already an invalid.'

'I was ill. But I never counted those years. I never said: "Now it is the month of Nisan again, but I am not blossoming again with the roses. Now it is Tishri and I still languish here." I went on speaking of Him both to myself and to good people. I realised that the years were

passing because the little ones of bygone days came to
bring me their wedding confections or the cakes for the
birth of their little ones. Now, if I look back, now that
from old I have become young, what do I see of my past?
Nothing. It is past.'

'Nothing here. But in Heaven it is "everything" for you,
Isaac, and that "everything" is waiting for you ' says
Jesus. And then speaking to everyone: 'You must do so.
I do so Myself. We must go on. Without getting tired.
Tiredness is one of the roots of human pride. And so
is haste. Why is man annoyed by defeats? Why is he
upset by delays? Because pride says: "Why say "no' to
me? So much delay for me? This is a lack of respect for
the apostle of God." No, My friends. Look at the whole
universe and think of Him Who made it. Meditate on
the progress of man and consider his origin. Think of
this hour which is now being completed and count how
many centuries have preceded it. The universe is the
work of a calm creation. The Father did not do things
in a disorderly way; He made the universe in successive
phases. Man is the work of patient progress, the present
man, and he will progress more and more in knowledge
and in power. And such knowledge and power will be
holy or not holy, according to his will. But man did not
become skilled all at once. The First Parents, expelled
from the Garden, had to learn everything, slowly,
progressively. They had to learn the simplest things:
that a grain of corn is tastier if ground into flour, then
kneaded and then baked. And they had to learn how
to grind it and bake it. They had to learn how to light a
fire. How to make a garment by observing the fleece of
animals. How to make a den by watching beasts. How

to build a pallet by watching nests. They learned how
to cure themselves with herbs and water by observing
animals that do so by instinct. They learned to travel
across deserts and seas, studying the stars, breaking
in horses, learning how to balance boats on water by
watching the shell of a nut floating on the water of a
stream. And how many failures before success! But
man succeeded. And he will go farther. But he will not
be happier on account of his progress because he will
become more skilled in evil than in good. But he will
make progress. Is Redemption not a patient work? It
was decided centuries and centuries ago. It is happening
now after being prepared for centuries. Everything is
patience. Why be impatient then? Could God not have
made everything in a flash? Was it not possible for man,
gifted with reason, created by the hands of God, to know
everything in a flash? Could I not have come at the
beginning of centuries? Everything was possible. But
nothing must be violence. Nothing. Violence is always
against order and God, and what comes from God is
order. Do not attempt to be superior to God.'
'But, then, when will You be known? '
'By whom, Judas? '
'By the world! '
'Never! '
'Never? But are You not the Saviour? '
'I am. But the world does not want to be saved. Only
one in a thousand will be willing to know Me and only
one in ten thousand will really follow Me. And I will say
even more; I will not be known even by My most intimate
friends.'
'But if they are Your intimate friends, they will know You.'

'Yes, Judas. They will know Me as Jesus, as Jesus
the Israelite. But they will not know Me as He Who I
am....' and with resigned discouragement, Jesus opens
His hands and holding the, out turned outwards, He
continues, with sorrow written on His face, looking at
neither man nor Heaven but only at His future destiny of
a betrayed person '...I solemnly tell you that I will not be
known by all My intimate friends. To know means to love
with loyalty and virtue... and there will be who does not
know Me.'

'Do not say that ' implores John.

'We follow You, to know You more and more ' says Simon,
and the shepherds in chorus.

'We follow You as we would follow a bride and You are
dearer to us than she could be; we are more jealous of
You than of a woman....' Says Judas '...Oh! no. We know
You already so much that we cannot ignore You any
longer.' and pointing at Isaac, Judas continues 'He says
that to deny Your remembrance of a New-Born Baby
would have been more distressing than losing his life.
And You were but a new-born baby. We know You as Man
and Master. We listen to You and see Your works. Your
contact, Your breath, Your kiss: they are our continuous
consecration and our continuous purification. Only a
satan could deny You after being Your close companion.'

'It is true, Judas. But there will be one.'

'Woe to him! I will be his executioner.'

'No. Leave justice to the Father. Be his redeemer. The
redeemer of this soul that is inclined towards Satan. But
let us say goodbye to Isaac. It is evening. I bless you, My
faithful servant. You now know that Lazarus of Bethany
is our friend and is willing to help My friends. I am going.

You are staying here. Prepare the parched land of Judaea for Me. I will come later. In case of need you know where to find Me. My peace be with you ' and Jesus blesses and kisses His disciple.

Jesus With The Shepherd Jonah In The Plain Of Esdraelon

It is night time but there is no relief from the great heat of the day as the still burning soil gives off bursts of heat from the furrows and the cracks in the soil that evaporate the dew even before it reaches the ground.

It is a clear night, although the setting moon is barely visible in the far east.

On a little stubble strewn path full of crickets and running between two parched fields, Jesus walks side by side with Levi and John. Behind them, in a group, are Joseph, Judas and Simon. Silently, they walk, hot and exhausted but Jesus smiles.

'Do You think he will be there? ' Jesus asks Levi.

'He will certainly be there. This is the time when the crops are stored away but they have not yet started picking the fruit. Farmers are therefore busy watching their vineyards and orchards against robbers and they do not go away, especially when their masters are as stingy as Jonah's. Samaria is not far and when those renegades get a chance... oh! they are happy to cause damage to us Israelites. Do they not know that the servants get beaten for it? Of course they do. But they hate us, that's all.'

'Do not cherish resentment, Levi ' says Jesus.

'No. But You will see how Jonah was wounded five years ago because of them. Since then he lives watching at night. Because the scourge is a cruel punishment...'

'Is there still a long way to go? '

'No, Master. See where this dreariness ends and there is a dark area? The orchards of Doras, the cruel Pharisee, are there. If You will allow me, I will go on in front of You to let Jonah hear me.'

'Yes, go.'

'Are all the Pharisees like that, my Lord? ' asks John.

'Oh! I would not like to be in their service! I prefer my boat.'

'Is your boat your dearest thing?' asks Jesus half seriously.

'No, You are! It was the boat when I did not know that Love was on the earth ' answers John promptly.

Jesus smiles at his impulsiveness. 'You did not know that love was on the earth? And how were you born then, if your father did not love your mother? ' asks Jesus, jokingly.

'That love is beautiful but it does not attract me. You are my love, You are the love on the earth for poor John.'

Jesus embraces him and says: 'I was anxious to hear you say so. Love is greedy for love and man gives and will always give tiny drops to its thirst, like these which are falling from the sky and are so small that they vanish mid-air in the great summer heat. Also man's drops of love will vanish mid-air, killed by the heat of too many things. Hearts will still squeeze them out... but interests, love, business, greed, so many human things will burn them. And what will rise to Jesus? Oh! too little! The remains, the few surviving human pulsations, men's

throbs interested in asking, asking, and asking in urgent
need. To love Me out of pure love will be the
characteristic of few people... of people like John...'
And Jesus stops before a thin ear of corn growing at the
edge of the foot path, in a little ditch that was perhaps a
little stream in the rainy weather.
'... Look at an ear of corn grown after the end of the
season. It is perhaps a seed that fell at harvest time. But
it was able to spring up, to resist sunshine and dry
weather, to grow up to form an ear... Feel it: it is already
formed. In these stripped fields it is the only living thing.
Before long the ripe grains will break the smooth husk
that holds them close to the stem and fall on the ground.
And they will become charity food for the little birds, or
yielding one hundred per cent, they will grow again and
before winter brings the plough back to the earth, they
will be ripe once again and will satisfy the hunger of
many birds already starving in the dreariest season...
See, My John, what one brave seed can do?
And the few people that will love Me out of pure love, will
be like that. One only will satisfy the hunger of many.
One only will make beautiful the area which before was
ugly. One only will give life where there was death and all
the hungry ones will come to that one. They will eat a
grain of its active love and then, selfish and absent-
minded, they will fly away. But also without their
knowing it, that grain will put vital germs in their blood,
in their souls... and they will come back. And today,
tomorrow and the day after, as Isaac said, the knowledge
of the Love will increase in their hearts. The stripped
stem will no longer be a living thing: a parched straw.
But how much good from its sacrifice! And how much

reward for its sacrifice! '

John listens with ardent admiration to Jesus and when
Jesus moves on, John follows Him. The group behind,
speaking among themselves , are unaware of the tender
conversation.

They arrive at the orchard, perspiring even though they
are not wearing mantles and stop in a silent group.
levi, visible in his light clothes, emerges from a dark
thicket faintly lit by moonlight. Behind him, another, in
a darker dress.

'Master, Jonah is here.'

'May My peace come to you!' greets Jesus before Jonah
reaches Him.

Jonah runs and throws himself weeping at His feet and
kisses them. When he is fit to speak he says: 'How long
have I waited for You! How long! How depressing it was to
feel that my life was passing away, that death was
approaching, and I had to say: "I have not seen Him!"
And yet, no, not all hopes were destroyed. Not even when
I was about to die. I would say: "She said so: 'You will
serve Him again' and She could not have said something
that was not true. She is the Mother of the Immanuel. No
one, therefore, possesses God more than She does and
who has God knows what is of God." '

'Get up. She sends you Her greetings. You have been
near Her and You are still near Her. She lives at
Nazareth.'

'You! She! At Nazareth? Oh! I wish I had known. At night,
in the cold winter months, when the fields rest and evil
people cannot cause damage to farmers, I would have
come, I would have run there to kiss Your feet and I

would have come back with my treasure of certainty of faith. Why did You not show Yourself, Lord?'

'Because it was not the time. The time has now come. We must learn to wait. You said: "In the winter months when the fields rest". And yet they have been sown have they not? Well, I was like a grain that had been sown. And you saw Me when I was being sown. Then I disappeared. Buried in necessary silence.

That I might grow and reach harvest time and shine in the eyes of the world and of those who had seen Me a New-Born Baby. That time has come. The New-Born is now ready to be the Bread of the world. And I am looking first for My faithful ones, and I say to them: "Come. I will satisfy your hunger." '

Jonah listens to Him, smiling happily and repeating to himself: 'Oh! You are really here! You are really here!'

'You were about to die? When?'

'When I was thrashed to death because they had stripped two vineyards. Look how many wounds! ' He lowers his tunic and shows his shoulders covered with irregular scars. 'He beat me with an iron rod. He counted the bunches of grapes that had been picked; he could see where the stalks had been torn off, and he gave me a blow for every bunch. And then he left me there, half dead. Mary helped me. She is the young wife of a friend of mine, and she has always been fond of me. Her father was the land agent before me and when I came here I became very fond of the little girl because her name was Mary. She took care of me and I recovered after two months, for the sores had become infected from the heat and had given me a high temperature. I said to the God of Israel: "It does not matter. Let me see Your Messiah

again and this misfortune is of no importance to me.
Accept it as a sacrifice. I can never offer You a sacrifice; I
am the servant of a cruel man and You know. He does
not even allow me to come to Your altar at Passover.
Accept me as a victim. But give me Him!" '
'And the Most High has satisfied you. Jonah, do you wish
to serve Me, as your friends are already doing?'
'Oh! How shall I do that?'
'As they do. Levi knows and he will tell you how simple it
is to serve Me. I only want your good will.'
'I have given You that since the time You cried in the
manger. It made me overcome everything. Both dejection
and hatred. The fact is... we cannot speak very much
here... The master once kicked me because I was
insisting that You existed. But when he was away, and
with those I could trust, oh! I did tell the wonder of that
night!'
'And now tell the wonder of your meeting. I have found
almost everyone and everyone is faithful. Is that not a
wonder? Only because you contemplated Me with faith
and love you have become just in the eyes of God and
men.'
'Oh! Now I will have courage! And how much courage!
Now that I know that You are alive I can say: "He is there.
Go to Him!..." But where, my Lord?'
'All over Israel. Up to September I will be in Galilee. I will
Often be at Nazareth or Capernaum, and I can be traced
from there. After... I will be everywhere. I have come to
gather the sheep of Israel.'
'Oh! My Lord! You will find many billy-goats. Beware of
the great ones in Israel!'
'They will not do Me any harm if it is not the time. Say to

the dead, the sleepers, the living: "The Messiah is
amongst us."'

'To the dead, Lord?'

'To those whose souls are dead. The others, the just who
died in the Lord, are already rejoicing for their imminent
liberation from Limbo. Say to the dead: "I am the Life."
Say to the sleepers: "I am the Sun that rises awaking
from sleep." Say to the living: "I am the Truth they are
seeking." '

'And You cure also sick people? Levi told me about Isaac.
Is the miracle only for him, because he is Your shepherd
or is it for everybody?'

'For good people, a miracle is a just reward. For those
who are not so good, it urges them toward true goodness.
It is also for bad people, to shake them and make them
understand that I Am and that God is with Me. A miracle
is a gift. Gifts are for good people. But He Who is Mercy
and sees the human burden, which can be lightened only
by powerful events, has resort also to this means, that
He may say: "I have done everything for you but all in
vain. Tell Me, therefore, what else I must do." '

'Lord, do You mind entering my house? If You give me
assurance that no robber will come into the estate, I
would like to give You hospitality, and invite also the few
people who know You because I spoke to them of You.
Our master has bent and broken us like inferior stems.
We have but the hope of an eternal reward. But if You
will show Yourself to downcast hearts, they will feel new
strength.'

'I will come. Do not be afraid for your trees and
vineyards. Can you believe that the angels will watch
them faithfully?'

'Oh! My Lord. I saw Your heavenly servants. I do believe. And I will come with You and feel safe. Blessed these trees and vineyards which have the breeze and songs of angelical wings and voices! Blessed is the soil which is sanctified by Your feet! Come, Lord Jesus! Listen, trees and vines. Listen, soil. Now I will say to Him the Name that I confided to you for my own peace. Jesus is here. Listen, and may the sap exult through branches and vine shoots. The Messiah is with us.'

Return To Nazareth After Leaving Jonah

It is time to say goodbye and Jesus and His disciples are standing at the door of a poor hut, with Jonah and other poor peasants, lit by a light so faint, it seems to be blinking.

'Will I not see You again, my Lord? ' asks Jonah. 'You have brought light to our hearts. Your kindness has turned these days into a feast that will last all our lives. But You have seen how we are treated. A mule is taken better care of than we are. And trees receive more human attention; they are money. We are only millstones that earn money and we are used until we die of excessive toil. But Your words have been as many loving caresses. Our bread seemed more plentiful and it tasted better because You shared it with us; this bread which he does not even give to his dogs. Come back to share it with us, my Lord. Only because it is You, I dare say that. It would be an insult to offer anyone else shelter and food which even a beggar would disdain. But You...'
'But I find in them a heavenly perfume and flavour because in them there is faith and love. I will come, Jonah. I will come back. You stay in your place, tied like

an animal to the shafts. May your place be Jacob's
ladder. And in fact angels go and come from Heaven
down to you, carefully gathering all your merits and
taking them up to God. But I will come to you. To relieve
your spirit. Be faithful to Me, all of you. Oh! I would like
to give you also human peace. But I cannot. I must say to
you: go on suffering. And that is very sad for One Who
loves...'

'Lord, if You love us, we no longer suffer. Before we had
no one to love us...Oh! If I could, at least, see Your
Mother! '

'Do not worry. I will bring Her to you. When the weather
is milder, I will come with Her. Do not risk incurring cruel
punishments on account of your anxiety to see Her. You
must wait for Her as you wait for the rising of a star, of
the evening star. She will appear to you all of a sudden,
exactly as the evening star, which is not there one
moment, and a moment later it shines in the sky. And
you must consider that even now She is lavishing Her
gifts of love on you. Goodbye, everybody. May My peace
protect you from the harshness of him who torments
you. Goodbye, Jonah. Do not cry. You have waited for so
many years with patient faith. I now promise you a very
short wait. Do not weep; I will not leave you alone. Your
kindness wiped My tears when I was a New-Born Baby.
Is Mine not sufficient to wipe yours?'

'Yes... but You are going away... and I have to remain
here...'

'Jonah, My friend, do not make Me go away depressed
because I cannot comfort you ...'

'I am not crying, my Lord... But how will I be able to live
without seeing You, now that I know that You are alive?'

Jesus caresses the forlorn old man once again and then goes away. But standing on the edge of the miserable threshing floor, Jesus stretches His arms out and blesses the country. Then He departs.

'What have You done, Master?' asks Simon who has noticed the unusual gesture. .

'I put a seal on everything. That no demon may damage things and thus cause trouble to those wretched people. I could do no more...'

'Master, let us walk on a little faster. I would like to tell You something which I do not want the others to hear. 'They move farther away from the group and Simon begins to speak: 'I wanted to tell You that Lazarus has instructions to use my money to assist all those who apply to him in Jesus' name. Could we not free Jonah? That man is worn out and his only joy is to be with You. Let us give him that. What is his work worth here? If instead he were free, he would be Your disciple in this beautiful yet desolate plain. The richest people in Israel own fertile estates here and they exploit them with cruel extortion, exacting a hundredfold profit from their workers. I have known that for years. You will not be able to stop here long, because the sect of the Pharisees rules over the country and I do not think it will ever be friendly to You. These oppressed and hopeless workers are the most unhappy people in Israel. Your heard it Yourself, not even at Passover have they peace, neither can they pray, whilst their severe masters, with solemn gestures and affected exhibitions, take up prominent positions in front of all the people. At least they will have the joy of knowing that You exist and of listening to Your words repeated to them by one who will not alter one single

letter. If You agree Master, please say so, and Lazarus will
do what is necessary.'

'Simon, I knew why you gave all your property away. The
thoughts of men are known to Me. And I loved you also
because of that. By making Jonah happy, you make
Jesus happy. Oh! How it torments Me to see good people
suffer! My situation of a poor man despised by the world
afflicts Me only because of that. If Judas heard Me, he
would say: "But are You not the Word of God? Give the
order and these stones will become gold and bread for
the poor people." He would repeat Satan's snare. I am
anxious to satisfy people's hunger. But not the way
Judas would like. You are not yet sufficiently mature to
grasp the depth of what I want to say. But I will tell you:
if God saw to everything He would rob His friends. He
would deprive them of the chance of being merciful and
fulfilling the commandment of love. My friends must
possess this mark of God in common with Him: the holy
mercy consisting in deeds and words. And the
unhappiness of other people gives My friends the
opportunity to practice it.
Have you understood what I mean?'

'Your thought is a deep one. I will ponder Your words.
And I humble myself as I see how dull-minded I am and
how great God is Who wants us to be gifted with all His
most sweet attributes so that He may call us His
children. God is revealed to me in His manifold
perfections by every ray of light with which You
illuminate my heart. Day by day, like one advancing in
an unknown place, the knowledge of the immense Thing
which is the Perfection Which wants to call us His
"children" progresses in me and I seem to climb like an

eagle or to dive like a fish into two endless depths like sky and sea, and I climb higher and higher and dive deeper and deeper but I never touch the end. But what is, therefore, God?'

'God is the unattainable Perfection, God is the perfect Beauty, God is the infinite Power, God is the incomprehensible Essence, God is the unsurpassable Bounty, God is the indestructible Mercy, God is the immeasurable Wisdom, God is the Love that became God. He is the Love! He is the Love! You say that the more you know God in His perfection, the higher you seem to climb and the deeper to dive into two endless depths of shadeless blue... But when you understand what is the Love that became God, you will no longer climb or dive into the blue but into a blazing vortex and you will be drawn towards a beatitude that will be death and life for you. You will possess God, with a perfect possession, when, by your will, you succeed in understanding and deserving Him. You will then be fixed in His perfection.'

'O Lord... ' exhales Simon, overwhelmed.

They walk in silence until they reach the road where Jesus stops to wait for the others.

When they regroup again, Levi kneels down: 'I should be leaving, Master. But Your servant asks You a favour. Take me to Your Mother. This man is an orphan like me. Do not deny me what You give him, that I may see the face of a mother...'

'Come. What is asked in My Mother's name, I grant in My Mother's name.'

The sun, although about to set, blazes down unto the grey- green dome of the thick olive trees laden with small

well- shaped fruit but only penetrates the tangle of
branches enough to provide a few tiny eyelets of light
whereas the main road, on the other hand, embedded
between two banks, is a dusty blazing dazzling ribbon.

Alone and walking fast among the olive trees, Jesus
smiles to Himself...He smiles even more happily when He
reaches a cliff....Nazareth....its panorama flickering in the
heat of the blazing sun...and Jesus begins to descend
and quickens His step.
Now on the silent, deserted road, He has protected His
head with His mantle and, no longer minding the sun, is
walking so fast that the mantle is blowing at His sides
and behind Him so that He seems to be flying.
Now and again, the voice of a child or of a woman from
inside a house or a kitchen garden reaches Jesus where
He is walking in the shady spots provided by garden trees
whose branches extend into the road. He turns into a
half shaded road where there are women gathered
around a cool well and they all salute Him, welcoming
Him in shrill voices.
'Peace to you all... But please be silent. I want to give My
Mother a surprise.'
'Her sister-in-law has just gone away with a pitcher of
cool water. But she is coming back. They are left without
any water. The spring is either dry or the water is
absorbed by the parched land before reaching Your
garden. We don't know. That's what Mary of Alphaeus
was saying. There she is... she is coming.'
Not having seen Jesus yet, the mother of Judas and
James, with an amphora on her head and another in her
hand, is shouting; 'I'll be quicker this way. Mary is very

sad, because Her flowers are dying of thirst. They are the ones planted by Joseph and Jesus and it breaks Her heart to see them withering.'

'But now that She sees Me... ' says Jesus appearing from behind the group of women.

'Oh! My Jesus! Blessed You are! I'll go and tell...'

'No. I will go. Give Me the amphoras.'

'The door is half shut. Mary is in the garden. Oh! How happy She will be! She was speaking of You also this morning. But why come in this heat! You are all perspiration! Are You alone?'

'No. With friends. But I came ahead of them to see My Mother first. And Judas?'

'He is at Capernaum. He often goes there.' says Mary. And she smiles as she dries Jesus' wet face with her veil. The pitchers now ready, Jesus takes two, tying one at each end of His belt which He throws across His shoulder and then takes a third one in His hand. Then He walks away, turns round a corner, reaches the house, pushes the door, enters the little room that seems dark in comparison with the bright sunshine outside. Slowly, He lifts the curtain at the garden door and He watches. Mary is standing near a rose-bush with Her back to the house, pitying the parched plant. Jesus lays the pitcher on the floor and the copper tinkles against a stone. 'Are you here already, Mary?' says His Mother without turning round.

'Come, come, look at this rose! And these poor lilies. They will all die if we do not assist them. Bring also some small canes to hold up this falling stalk.'

'I will bring You everything, Mother.'

Mary springs round and for a moment, She remains with

119

Her eyes wide open then with a cry She runs with
outstretched arms towards Her Son, Who has already
opened His arms and is waiting for Her with the most
loving smile.

'Oh! My Son!'

'Mother! Dear!'

Their embrace is a long and loving one and Mary is so
happy that She does not feel how hot Jesus is. But then
She notices it: 'Why, Son, did You come at this time of
the day? You are purple red and perspiring like a sodden
sponge. Come inside. That I may dry and refresh You. I
will bring You a fresh tunic and clean sandals. My Son!
My Son! Why go about in this heat! The plants are dying
because of the heat and You, My Flower, are going about.'

'It was to come to You as soon as possible, Mother.'

'Oh! My dear! Are You thirsty? You must be. I will now
prepare...'

'Yes, I am thirsty for Your kisses, Mother. And for Your
caresses. Let Me stay like this, with My head on Your
shoulder, as when I was a little boy... Oh! Mother! How I
miss You!'

'Tell Me to come, Son, and I will. What did You lack
because of My absence? The food You like? Clean
clothes? A well-made bed? Oh! My Joy, tell Me what You
lacked. Your servant, My Lord, will endeavour to provide.'

'Nothing, but You...'

Hand in hand, Mother and Son go into the house. Jesus
sits on the chest near the wall, embraces Mary Who is in
front of Him, resting His head on Her heart and kissing
Her now and again. Now He stares at Her: 'Let Me look at
You to My heart's content, holy Mother of Mine.'

'Your tunic first. It is not good for You to remain so damp.

Come. ' Jesus obeys. When He comes back wearing a fresh looking tunic, they resume their sweet conversation.

'I have come with My disciples and friends but I left them in Melcha's wood. They will come tomorrow at dawn. I... I could not wait any longer. My Mother!... ' and He kisses Her hands. 'Mary of Alphaeus has gone away to leave us alone. She also understood how anxious I was to be with You. Tomorrow...tomorrow You will attend to My friends and I to the Nazarenes. But this evening You are My Friend and I am Yours. I brought You... Oh! Mother: I found the shepherds of Bethlehem. And I brought You two of them: they are orphans and You are the Mother of all men. And more so of orphans. And I brought You also one who needs You to control himself. And another one who is a just man and has suffered so much. And then John... And I brought You the recollections of Elias, Isaac, Tobias, now called Matthew, John and Simeon. Jonah is the most unhappy of them all. I will take You to him... I promised him. I will continue to look for the others. Samuel and Joseph are resting in the peace of God.'

'Were You at Bethlehem?'

'Yes, Mother. I took there the disciples who were with Me. And I brought You these little flowers, that were growing near the stones of the threshold.'

'Oh! ' Mary takes the withered stems and kisses them. 'And what about Anne?'

'She died in Herod's slaughter.'

'Oh! Poor woman! She was so fond of You!'

'The Bethlehemites suffered a lot. But they have not been fair to the shepherds. But they suffered a lot...'

'But they were good to You then!'

'Yes. And that is why they are to be pitied. Satan is jealous of their past kindness and urges them to evil things. I was also at Hebron. The shepherds, persecuted...'

'Oh! To that extent?!'

'Yes, they were helped by Zacharias, who got them jobs and food, even if their masters were hard people. But they are just souls and they turned their persecutions and wounds into merits of true holiness. I gathered them together. I cured Isaac... and I gave My name to a little boy... At Juttah, where Isaac was languishing and where he came back to life again, there is now an innocent group, called Mary, Joseph and Jesai...'

'Oh! Your Name!'

'And Yours and the name of the Just One. And at Kerioth, the fatherland of a disciple, a faithful Israelite died resting on My heart. Out of joy, having found Me... And then... Ah! how many things I have to tell You, My perfect Friend, sweet Mother! But first of all, I beg You, I ask You to have so much mercy on those who will be coming tomorrow. Listen: they love Me... but they are not perfect. You, Teacher of virtue... oh! Mother, help Me to make them good... I would like to save them all...' Jesus has slipped at Mary's feet. She now appears in Her Motherly majesty.

'My Son! What do You want Your poor Mother to do better than You do?'

'To sanctify them... Your virtue sanctifies. I brought them here deliberately, Mother... one day I will say to You: "Come", because it will then be urgent to sanctify souls, that I may find them willing to be redeemed. And I will

123

not be able by Myself... Your silence will be as eloquent
as My words. Your purity will assist My power. Your
presence will keep Satan away... and Your Son, Mother,
will feel stronger knowing that You are near Him. You will
come, will you not, My sweet Mother?'
'Jesus! Dear Son! I have a feeling that You are not
happy... What is the matter, Creature of My heart? Was
the world hostile to You? No? It is a relief to believe it...
but... Oh! Yes. I will come. Wherever You wish, as and
when You wish. Even now, in this blazing sunshine, or by
night, in cold or wet weather. You want Me? Here I am.'
'No. Not now. But one day... How sweet is our home. And
Your caresses! Let Me sleep thus, with My head on Your
knees. I am so tired! I am still Your little Son... ' And
Jesus really falls asleep, tired and exhausted, sitting on
the mat, His head on the lap of His Mother, Who happily
caresses His hair.

www.ingramcontent.com/pod-product-compliance
Lightning Source LLC
Chambersburg PA
CBHW060021050426
42448CB00012B/2831